First edition, 2025

Copyright © 2025 Shomendra Mann

This autobiography is published under the terms of the Author's Proprietary License. It is protected by international copyright law—including the Berne Convention for the Protection of Literary and Artistic Works—and by applicable national statutes (for example, the U.S. Copyright Act of 1976).

No part of this work may be reproduced, distributed, transmitted, or stored in any form or by any means—whether electronic, mechanical, photocopying, recording, or otherwise—without the prior express written permission of the author. Unauthorized use or distribution of this material is strictly prohibited and may result in legal action.

CHRONICLES

Introduction	2
Growing Up	5
Starting the Civilian Life	19
Finding Our Feet	26
Going To Market	35
The Russian Adventure	45
The Equipment Worked!	56
To Climb a Mountain	66
Life is Beautiful	78
Singapore Calling	82
The Bucket and The Oven	89
To Save a Penny	94
Growing The Company	108
Annexure	118

I

INTRODUCTION

Unwrapped Wishes is about how a retired Army colonel and his three brats created a world-class company, Amchem, with zero capital or business background. Today, we are considered among the best in the world in terms of products, technologies, and capability in producing solvent-free polyurethane coatings. Since these are high-end, niche products for the moment, we are not a huge company; we are just the best.

The purpose behind writing this book is to tell people with dreams that it is possible to go from nothing to something if you put your heart on it. When you start in life and look at all the successful people: businesspeople, scientists, artists, historians, and educationists, you may think they're all very different from you or have something you don't have. That is not true. They started just the same way as you are starting now. How did they convert their dreams to reality? If I could inspire some people and change their lives, the purpose of this book would be served. It can be done!

I have been greatly inspired by one book I read early in my life, *The Law of Success* by Napoleon Hill. I found this gem in my father's books as an early teen and read it out of curiosity. It seemed very dated, but it ignited a spark in my mind. The fundamentals of human nature never really change, and what was valid when Napoleon Hill wrote the book is still valid today. Everyone should get a copy of that book and read it. The book I am starting today is not based on what Hill wrote but on my life experiences and the lessons I learned.

I have often thought about the purpose of life. On the face of it, there is none. We are just another living being; we are born, grow up, procreate, age, and eventually die. Nothing we do serves a purpose in this immense universe. Even the universe and life itself do not seem to have a purpose. The question then arises: why should we strive to achieve something? Why should we not then live an ordinary life and get by? Most living beings are doing just that, which is completely fine. To provide yourself with challenges and achieve those results in great satisfaction and a sense of purpose in life.

I will narrate this book from my viewpoint because it is much simpler. I will not be delving into my personal life except where it is relevant to the story.

The story of Amchem is not my story but the story of my Father, Colonel Mann, my two brothers, Raj and Deepender, and me. Father is a distinguished officer from the Indian army and a war veteran. He also always nursed a dream inside to create a business. When he took premature retirement from the Indian army due to an accident (and medically downgraded), he could have moved to a small town and lived the rest of his life at leisure. Instead, at age 47, he moved his family lock, stock, and barrel to a big city, New Delhi, to start a business with zero capital and experience. It was a gutsy move. This brings us to the first lesson: if you want to do something in life, you cannot hesitate too much; jump into the water!

We three boys were in high school, and had it not been for the shift, we would have gone on to different careers. I always had a scientific bent of mind, so I would have gone into research. Thankfully, as an owner of a business, I can now do as much research as I want on the subjects that I like. Today, my greatest satisfaction comes not from the money I earn but rather from the products I develop. There is nothing like the thrill of making something new and unique.

Why did I write the Annexure?

When I was a child, I read The Emperor's New Clothes. It was a simple story about a foolish ruler tricked into believing he was wearing magical clothes—invisible clothes. Afraid of looking unworthy, he pretended to see them. His ministers did the same. No one wanted to admit the truth until a child finally pointed out what was obvious: the emperor wasn't wearing anything at all.

I realized this story wasn't just about an emperor as I grew older. It was about all of us. We live in a world where people often pretend things are fine, even when they're not. We've made huge progress—better technology, medicine, and comforts than ever before. But at the same time, we face big problems. Politics has become more about winning than serving the people. The gap between the rich and the poor keeps growing. Our justice system is slow and unfair. We're destroying our environment in the name of progress. And instead of bringing people together, social media divides us.

Despite all this, many of us, like the emperor, choose to look the other way. It's easier to stay silent than to believe someone else will fix things. But if we don't face these problems now, they will only get worse.

This book is about my journey, but it's also about looking at these issues honestly. I don't have all the answers, but I want to share my thoughts on what could change. If we want a better world, we must speak up like the child in the story. It's time to see things as they really are.

II
Growing Up

Nothing to complain about here! I had the most fantastic childhood. We are the original Gen X Army brats, princes of the cantonment. Completely unsupervised with no helicopter parents. Our childhood revolved around sprawling bungalows, school, friends, sports clubs, and adventure. I couldn't care less about money and wealth. The adventure was wild and sometimes borderline foolish. Dad was posted every couple of years in a new town, which meant new friends, surroundings, and new areas to explore. It taught us to adapt to new situations and not depend on comfort. My mom and dad never knew precisely which grade we were in. We were supposed to handle situations in school and life, sink or swim. Parents nowadays are making a big mistake in planning and supervising every aspect of their children's lives. They make every decision for the child and try to make life as comfortable as possible. I can understand the motivation; everyone does it, but it's a counterproductive step. Adversity and challenge appear regularly in life, and we must be equipped to handle them independently. Living a cocooned childhood deprives us of learning very valuable life skills.

Dad is by far the most incredible human I have ever met. Everyone around me feels the same, so it's not just my reaction as a son. He has loved and cared for every person in his life. I just don't get it. How can someone have so much empathy? If I had half of that, I would be blessed. But I did get a great set of morals and ethics from him. I refused to do many corrupt things people wanted and expected me to do and continued to resist. What are the points of cheating and winning? You always know inside that you are a cheat and not a winner. I would rather be the latter. If you achieve, money automatically follows.

Dad had a very privileged upbringing as the son of a landlord farmer. My grandfather owned about 2000 acres of land, sugar factory and all, yet managed to give away a large part in charity and to set up schools. I had the good fortune to visit my ancestral village some years ago, and the reception gave me a sense of coming from royalty. Whenever I have travelled to the towns of Punjab and met the hardy rural folk, I can sense the great values they hold inside. It shows in the philanthropy, which we all need to emulate. Dad never inherited the wealth due to some machinations, which I will not go into. Had that happened, we would have been enormously wealthy from the onset.

My dad was educated at home, with a teacher visiting him daily. It's challenging to play hooky! A student from an Ivy League would have a tough time keeping up with his knowledge and thirst for learning. So, subconsciously, that was a great lesson in my life. Learning does not begin or end in educational institutions. We need to learn all through our lives. More on this later.

Mom was always the practical one. But equally gifted. She handled three brats, housework, hobbies like painting, cooking, clubs, social life, and side businesses, all with such aplomb and energy. I laugh when people complain that they do not have time for this or that. You should have seen my mom in action. Nothing seemed to be tough for her. With a smile, she did everything in a breeze. During our road trips, she would unpack the cooking gear, cut vegetables, make dough for rotis (bread), and make a fresh hot lunch. There was no kitchen, just the roadside. I love tough people. Life is supposed to be lived this way: guts and glory, no self-pity and whining.

Coming from these two great people, no wonder my brothers grew up in the way they did. Raj was always the doer of the boys. Social with a long list of friends and a winner in all sports. Very competitive. He was in the Indian school teams (KV Sangathan) in six sports. We were following and trailing the head honcho. Dimple was the 'couldn't care less' one as a kid, and really funny. Exceptionally gifted in taking things apart to fix them. This skill set followed him through life, and so did his attitude.

Me, I was the dreamer. Constantly daydreaming and lost within myself. I was obsessed with science and would dwell on every word written in textbooks. I couldn't get enough. I used to interchangeably solve calculus with trigonometry, which gave me a high. Not to say I was a nerd. Pretty girls were another fascinating subject. And music. I would endlessly hear all the great music and follow all the Top 20's on the radio. While I used to play hockey, cricket, and football, I excelled in volleyball and table tennis during my teen years. I lived inside for a long time till I shifted to the outside world! Total introvert to situationally extrovert.

Fortunately, I have been gifted with a photographic memory, so I can vividly recall incidents and events of my childhood. Writing them down would require an entirely new book. I plan to do this to reminisce about my old years, but I will also share it with my family and close friends if they want to read my long story.

After teasing you, I would be amiss if I did not share just some of these experiences, so let's dive in.

Circa 1972

I was seven years old. We were staying at a place called Nasirabad in Rajasthan. Our house was just on the edge of this tiny town. Beyond our house started the wild desert of Rajasthan. The posting was mid-term, so we joined a school close to our home till the end of the term. The school comprised four large tents with subdivisions to house different classrooms. Voices from each classroom would carry over to the next, across the thin canvas walls, so we were getting simultaneously educated on various subjects and grades! There was a small lake on the way back home with alligators. That was so much fun to watch. In about six months, we transferred to St. Anselm's in Ajmer, about an hour's drive in the rear of a 3-ton truck. I don't remember much of that fancy school except for the ride on the way and back through the wild desert. Puts essential things in perspective.

The fun thing to do after school and on holidays was wander into the desert for hours. We quickly realized that the desert is not devoid of animal life. Hedgehogs, rabbits, snakes, and scorpions were abundant. We had a couple of cute hedgehogs as pets. The way to catch snakes and scorpions is to look under rocks and catch them off guard. One of us would lift the rock from the opposite side, and the other would be ready to push the head down with a wishbone stick. Bam. We would keep them in glass jars nicked from the kitchen. I don't know if the snakes were poisonous, and luckily, we didn't get bitten to find out! The scorpions were fascinating creatures. We once buried some of them in empty jam glass jars for months as a "scientific experiment." Lo and behold, the guys were alive when we took them out.

The place was fun, even though we had no TV or such entertainment. Our vagabond dog Tiffy would go on his sojourns for days together into the wild. Each time, the three of us would sit on the veranda looking at the desert sunset, praying for his return. Like a bad penny, he always did, bruised and battered after battling God knows what creature. Boy, did he have a personality?

Another pastime was to make a mickey out of the tuition teacher. Poor guy. He would come in a ramshackle cycle, circular cap, and gigantic spectacles. He would keep All pins pushed into the cap from the top edges for reasons only known to him. He would park the cap on the table. When he moved to the restroom, we removed the pins from the side and put them in the center. Ouch, that must have hurt when he put it back on. Also, his specs were coated with snot during the restroom break. He would start wondering about his vision loss when he put them back on. But the ultimate prank we played was with his cycle. The guy did not know how to get on the bike, so he installed a giant axle bolt on the rear wheel. He would trot alongside the bike, put one step on the bolt, and hop on. Two of us feigned illness one day, went out the back door, and reversed the axle bolt. He did the usual, but his foot didn't find anything there, so he went for a giant toss. Old man, please don't file a complaint in heaven now that you know who did that. We are sorry for that prank.

Timelapse to 1977

We drove from Jaipur to Raydak Tea Estate in Jalpaiguri, a 1000-mile drive to meet up with all cousins for a vacation—boiling summer in a Fiat Premier with no air conditioning. We were gung-ho, but the car used to pack up in the 45C heat and refuse to move. We even tried putting wet towels on the distributor, but she was not cooperating. So, we decided to rest during the day and drive at night. Dad used to drive about 300 miles each night in the pitch dark through the most remote, single-lane roads with blinding lights of incoming trucks. We reached the Simplipal jungle in Orissa and stopped at a forest rest house for the day.

I've never experienced such a miserable weather. It was hotter than hell, and the humidity was off the charts. The pores on our skin became huge with sebum production, and the skin got oily. Even the leaves of trees were about 5 feet wide to cool off. We saw tribals walk in the pitch dark at 3:00 AM, traveling about 20 miles to reach the regional market in the morning. It's a daily routine. Boy, these guys are tough. A city slicker would be dead after 3 miles in that weather. Our country is such a grave contrast, and it's a shame that many of us live comfortable lives while millions of our fellow humans continue to live miserable lives. We have lost every shred of empathy. Having traveled the length and breadth of the interiors of this country, I have no doubts that we need to wake up and wake up fast, or the wind will blow away these sandcastles. Our government should pour most of its resources into the vast poor population, not the cities, to create faux development. People in the cities have found their feet long ago, and private enterprises can pay for their glitzy lives.

Coming back to the journey. After dinner, as we are about to continue our journey, we ask the caretaker about the condition of the road ahead. Remember, our only GPS was the big Automobile Association book with hand-drawn maps. The dude says it's fine except for a slight stretch. I doubt if he had even gone beyond his village. After entering the jungle, the road decides to disappear completely. We are on a mountain track with boulders, in the thick jungle with no road, and a highly protesting Fiat regretting her date of manufacture. The car decides to go backward since it does not have enough energy to go up. Raj and I were tasked with going out and walking behind with large stones in our hands. We put stones behind the rear tires when the Fiat wants to collapse and retreat. All this was keenly watched by animal eyes that shone in the night, laughing away at our ordeal. It was tiger, bear, and elephant country. It took us 8 hours to move 12 miles across the hills.

Finally, we got to flat land and drove past a signboard—still thick jungle and narrow road. Since we could not reverse, Dad told Dimple to check out the sign. Mom started going berserk on how much danger is out there. What happens next is a life lesson. Dad calmly puts his hand into the dashboard drawer, pulls out his service gun, and hands it over to Dimple. He said now go, and he went. After about 5 minutes, he came running back, huffing and puffing, and Dad asked him what the sign said. "Beware of Bears," said Dimple .... Raj and I just cracked up.

The Wonder Years: 1978 – 1980

Ahmednagar was the training center of the Armoured Corps. Dad was initially posted as the Dy. Commandant. We were newly graduated teens, and it was one of the best times of our lives. We lived in a 3-acre British bungalow with a west wing for parents, an east wing for the brats, a vast lawn in front with a fishpond, and a rear side big enough to grow wheat. We went to the house's west side thrice in two years. Our school, Kendriya Vidyalaya, was a mile walk across wet grassland with angry-looking buffaloes with massive horns grazing. There was a narrow creek with some stones to step over. The trick to avoid getting gored by the buffaloes is to ignore them and not look them in the eye. The soil was like clay, which would stick to our shoes, and on some wet days, it became terrible. After months, we got fed up with removing the clay and started taking the longer route to school on our cycles.

The Army club, social hotspot, and sports center were called the Annexe. We would reach there right after school and return as late as possible. Amongst my friends were Sanjay, Sandeep, Kuldeep, and Rajendra, but my closest friend

Unwrapped Wishes

was Tubby. Together, we were like Tom and Jerry, hilarious and crazy. I also had funny, gutsy, and fabulous girls as friends: Vijaya, the stunning beauty with the aura of a Hollywood diva; Amita, my table tennis buddy; Tunty, my class buddy; and Sonia, her fun and outgoing sister. The closest friendships are the ones made in formative years. People liked you for who you were, not your social status, possible contacts, or potential Facebook posts. What happened to us all?

Tom & Jerry's antics in school were the stuff of legends. There are too many to recount here. Let me do one. One morning, I'm setting up the mic for the school. The whole school is in front of us, in lines waiting for the boring morning stuff. So, many kids are from low-income families, but they were some of my best buds. Their language was 'different'. One of them sets up a challenge for an abusive competition against the principal on the mike since it's off. My turn came, and I've always been very competitive and must win at everything. So, I thought about the stuff my buds speak and gave my best shot at the principal's mother. Suddenly, I saw horror on the faces of the whole school. Someone had turned on the mic. Tubby, if it was you, I'll meet you in hell and turn your mic on when you are bitching about the guy in charge. Anyway, I was suspended, pending expulsion, but the entire class stood up for me. They went to the principal and said if you expel him, we will all quit school. That worked. I felt awful for my actions, especially being the commandant's son. Black sheep feeling, I think, did a lot of baa, baa, and other forms of wailing.

Although I was good at studies, the consensus amongst the teachers was that Tubby and I would fail the board exams because we spent all our time in antics. Tubby was not so good in studies and barely passed. When the time came for the 10th boards, we decided to show them. We would study for many hours during the day and then all night with coffee breaks and midnight walks in the stadium across from our houses. Later, I realized that studying late in the night is the wrong way. The mind is most alert when fully rested during early morning hours, and nights are meant for sleep. Nonetheless, we gave it our all for 30 days. I would painstakingly make notes, which he would read and memorize. Then, we would write answers repeatedly. Writing the answer is the only way to ensure you have learned the subject. Well, when the result came out, I had topped the school, and Tubby came third. Everyone was stunned. The erstwhile topper started crying.

Tubby had this great habit of making 'To Do' lists for everything. I learned this from him, which would become invaluable later in life. Despite his moderate efforts at studies, Tubby went on to be a great success in life as CEO of major international travel companies. I attribute this to his focus, and I'm sure the famous 'To Do' lists were a major contributing factor.

Our gang of seven used to do weekend camping trips in the countryside. With deep, blue, crystal-clear water, Mula Dam was about an hour away. We got dropped on a Friday into the remote wilderness with tents and fishing gear—no food except some wheat flour and sugar for making a dessert (halwa). The idea was to catch Mahseer fish and survive on that for three days. Frying pans and oil were ready. Well, it turns out these guys are not easy to catch! We cast and reeled until our arms were off the socket, but there were no bites. The only thing that bit the lures and spoons were the rocks. I had to do a deep dive to retrieve them as we had a limited supply. Once, it got stuck near the sluice gates, which was a little scary retrieval. I could see the guys waving and screaming from the distance; apparently, a snake was swimming by. I looked up and saw the colossal sluice gate towering over me. My only thought was it opening and me getting swept away, tumbling hundreds of feet down the spillway.

The halwa was a disaster; we were used to eating but not cooking. We didn't know the flour was supposed to be cooked before putting in the water and sugar. It looked like glue, and we dumped it into the lake—a last meal for the fish. We then went skinny dipping in the beautiful sunset and crashed out for the night. It was an amazing starry night. The next day was a repeat, and we were starving. Still no food. By late afternoon, we were desperate. We sent a team of two to walk to the local village to get some food. Sanjay started pleading with the villagers for food, saying we hadn't eaten in days. Dimple promptly gave him a whack for begging, and they returned. To be fair to Sanjay, asking for things without paying is begging. Guess what, that night we made the glue again and ate it. When you are hungry, everything tastes good. On the third day, we were rescued by the return truck late in the afternoon and came back home. We gave tall tales of our tasty Mahseer to our folks back home and then went on to finish all the food in the house!

Another trip was to Kapurwadi Lake. This time we did not trust the fishing, so Tubby nicked his dad's 0.22 rifle and put an empty hockey stick in the fabric case as a decoy. This time, the plan was to shoot ducks and eat them. Since we were cycling down to the lake and had a lot of camping gear, he also 'borrowed' his dad's golf cart, which we towed behind one of the cycles. About 3 miles down, the wheels came apart, and Tubby started throwing a fit. His dad was a tall guy, 6'2", very strict, and used to give it off to Tubby regularly. We somehow made it to the lake after transferring the gear onto other bikes!

Well, it turns out that the ducks are very shifty characters, just like Daffy. They can spot a gun from a mile away and move to the other side. Also, the weapon to use is a 12 bore with a widespread and not a rifle. Even on the scope, they were like a speck of dirt from that distance, so the bullets kept whizzing past them. It's not a surprise that we went hungry again. But the wilderness was lovely. We kept turns watching throughout the night, armed with the 0.22 since the village was not too far off. The following day, we went to the local well for a bath. We peer inside and, lo and behold, see fish swimming on the top. Took the gun, and bam, bam. Killed about half a dozen. The issue now was how to get them out. Well, don't underestimate us. Raj took the ropes from the tent; we tied them together and climbed about 40 feet to get them. Getting back up was a lot tougher! Finally, we had something to eat. It wasn't very tasty, as we had only salt and chili powder, but it was enough for the day.

We returned to the well the following day, but no more fish could be seen and were probably alerted by Daffy Duck. By night, we were crazy hungry and cribbing like hell. So, our friend Rajendra Dangwal offers to ride back to his house in the pitch dark and get food. A 12-mile round trip in the pitch-dark country tracks. It was wild but a height of bravery. It took him about 4 hours for the return trip. We had all placed bets on whether he would return alive or not, which was mean in hindsight. We ate at 2 AM and crashed out. It was a perfect ending to a perfect day.

I've always been in love with nature and wildlife. I can't get enough and am happiest in my natural surroundings. I've been lucky to have stayed and traveled across the length and breadth of India and many parts of the world with my family. I have always marveled at the sheer beauty of the world, whether it be the crystal-clear waters of the deep ocean, the crisp air of the mountains, the thick jungles, or the desolate desert. It has been one of the big joys of my life.

Nature is wonderful. Humans have destroyed most of the wildlife and desecrated the land. Left to me, I would isolate vast tracks of land and get every human out of there—much more than the wildlife sanctuaries. Every animal, bird, insect, plant or shrub, and marine life has equal rights as humans to live. We have been around much less than them and have less of a right to this amazing thing we call nature. We must desperately preserve and maintain. What a shame to create concrete cities and call this development. I fear humans will run over, occupy, and spoil every place of beauty. I can already see it coming slowly and surely.

Unwrapped Wishes

I would be amiss to talk about Ahmednagar and not talk about the fantastic people of the services I met as an army brat. Tough, disciplined, upright and moral. Very cultured, colorful, and full of character. The bond between the officers and their families was so strong. The club had many social get-togethers, and everyone was dressed to the nines. Then there were the sporting gymkhanas, open-air movie nights, and hunting and fishing trips. Magical times and a different world altogether.

Our awkward teen socials were so much fun. We had afternoon dance parties since the girls were not allowed after 8:00 PM. We would have to paper over all the windows to create an impression of nighttime. After each dance, the boys and girls would retreat to separate sides. It was hilarious.

To the Army children, life was only fun and games. That is not true for the fathers. From a distance, tanks seem very cool. We attended a tank firing at one of the ranges (KK), where about ten were lined up and shooting at targets at about 1-3 miles. Families were invited, too, but we were seated about 100 yards away. The sound of firing was deafening, to say the least. For some seconds, you lose your hearing. The orange-red shells can be seen flying into the distance and hitting targets. What an experience. The operators inside must feel it even more despite their earmuffs. That's when you realize the power of these bad boys. Dad told me the unvarnished truth of how rough and cruel the war was and what a toll the sounds of explosions and lack of sleep took on their physical and mental health. He said that you could fry an egg on the tanks in the hot summer desert.

I remember the events of the 1971 war as seen from the viewpoint of the families left behind by the soldiers. We were in Ambala then, and there were daily air raids and bunker nights in pitch dark. The cantonment was very close to the Air Force base and subject to heavy bombing by the Pakistani Air Force. We could have been collateral damage. Mom must have been stressed since Dad was at the frontline in the pitch of the battle. We were young boys, enjoying all the action back home. Once, we saw an aircraft hit in the night, burst into flames, and crash at some distance. Promptly in the morning, we went on cycles with spanners and wrenches to get parts but could never find it. Later, we were told it had crashed about 25 miles away.

During the melee of one daytime aid raid, everyone ran helter-skelter and hid wherever they could. We were outside spotting the jets and saw that the candy vendor had left his cycle unattended. We promptly filled our woolen caps with whatever we could fit and had a gala time. Of course, he came to our house the next day, got paid for all the loot, and we got the boot.

III
Starting the Civilian Life

The word "civilian" brings back some laughs. One day, Tiffy, our dog, was attacked by other dogs outside our house. My mom questioned our Batman, who they belonged to. Mam," They were civilian dogs," he replied. In the eyes of army men, any outsider is a civilian.

In 1980 Dad retired prematurely and shifted us lock, stock, and barrel to New Delhi. We had looked at places to stay on the map and zoned in on Shanti Niketan, Vasant Vihar, or West End, conveniently located near potential schools. We set out to look at suitable houses. Wait a minute. The houses were nice enough, but were they rentals for one month or a year? Shock and awe.

We settled for a more affordable 3-bedroom, drawing-dining house floor in Greater Kailash 2 (Masjid Moth): shock and awe, part deux. The house was so tiny by our (army) standards. The whole house would fit in one of our sprawling bedrooms in Ahmednagar. And where were the lawns? It became a joke among the boys not to breathe in too deep, or there would be a vacuum in the house. To our credit, we quickly became used to the new lifestyle.

Dimple and I enrolled in Army Public School, Dhaula Kuan, and Raj in Bhagat Singh College. Based on my class in 10th grade, I was also accepted into Modern School Barakhamba but was discouraged by, surprise surprise, the principal himself. He said in not so many words that the students there were affluent, spoilt brats and that I would be better off in APS.

I initially faced ragging in APS, which was a new experience. I had always been the offender, not the offended (I just learned that offendee is not an actual word). But I quickly made some great friends: Mini, Ranjit, Aditi, Manraj, Shelly, and Esha. Mini was so much fun and lively, and she was a complete chatterbox. She took me into the cool kids' group and kept joking about the favour she had done. We had such a blast together, bunking and going to Chanakya Cinema, followed by lunches in Narula's and roaming around Connaught Place and every other market. Except for Aditi, who disappeared completely, we found each other on Facebook. Ranjit has been a wonderful friend, although we were a little competitive in school. He moved to the US shortly after school, and many decades later, I got a call one evening, and we chatted for quite a while. It was so nice to connect again, and it felt like no time had passed since we met 25 years ago. He has always been warm and welcoming, and he even drove us to Niagara from New York for a fantastic weekend.

Dad partnered with a businessman from Kolkata, who a mutual friend introduced. He had an office on the rooftop in the K block of Connaught Place. We had stayed there for a month when house hunting. I became so comfortable with the place I started thinking of the place as my second home. Later, I would attend college for some hours, return to my dad's office, and spend the rest of the day thinking up business ideas. Dad's partner was into merchant exports and had a company called Jaggi Brothers. Dad burned the midnight oil, trying to export handicrafts, hard goods, and every other possible traditional Indian export.

Unwrapped Wishes

In late 1982, I was tasked with sending telex messages to international prospects, which my dad used to draft and give to me. We did not have a machine, so Dad asked a neighbour to let us use his machine. The first time I went across the road to get the message made, I was told that their daughter knew how to operate the machine and for me to wait a while till she returned from the market. In came the most beautiful and gentle girl, Neelu, who became the love of my life and my wife. She is the most wonderful person I've ever known, and we have had the most fantastic life together. She is tough as nails on the outside yet very caring and giving to everyone. I've seen her go to work with a 104°F fever without complaining. She has faced many difficulties in life with a smile and an indomitable spirit. Most upright and honest, in the 42 years I've known her, she has never told a lie and given me a reason to lower my eyes. I've been genuinely blessed if the adage behind every man ... is true.

After school, I enrolled in St. Stephen's College to take a course in chemistry. I had a natural liking for the subject and had scored a perfect 100 in my school pre-board. By this time however, I had lost interest in theoretical studies and was itching to start working. Attending every day was tough, but I did and finished my undergraduate course since I was never a quitter. Thank God to my best buddies, Sunil Jasuja and Pankaj Jain, who allowed me to spend my non-class time at the college without being bonkers.

St. Stephen's College is an excellent institution with terrific kids, but I wanted to get to the real world quickly. Looking back, my professors did a great job, and I got a good understanding of the fundamentals of Chemistry, despite my best efforts, which would be very useful later in life. Dr. Maini and Dr. Frank were chilled-out guys and my favorites, although in hindsight, Dr. Eswaran, our strict head of department, was the most talented and inspiring. I'm pretty sure they hated me since I had the attitude of a gangster, wore the shortest sleeveless shirts to show my biceps, was probably the only one who smoked, and wasn't deferential. The other kids in my class were angels in comparison.

Shomendra Mann

I would look forward to going to my dad's office for the rest of the day and return home with him. I quickly developed a keen interest in international business and would go to libraries of Trade Fair Authorities to collect names and addresses of global customers. Even then, I aimed big and wrote letters to the top companies, Neiman Marcus, Macy's, and the like, offering them products from India. I typed all the letters, signed them, put them in an envelope, affixed the stamps, and dropped them off at the post office. I never got a single reply, but to an 18-year-old, it was an incredible high. I honed my letter-writing and formatting skills and found the concept fascinating. It started dawning on me that this was my calling after all.

My mom's uncle was a successful, self-made industrialist from Kolkata who owned Pullmann Engineering company. He was a fascinating character. He was very serious in his home but extremely outgoing when away. Wherever we were posted and he was traveling to the vicinity, he would make it a point to visit us. What a laugh riot. I had always been in awe of his factories, huge homes, power, and wealth, which he had created from scratch. He even owned a personal Cessna aircraft, which he used to fly. I had heard stories of him starting by making welding rods himself. My maternal grandfather also had a factory but was not as successful as his brother. In hindsight, my ambitions at business were partly inspired by the story of my mom's Uncle. I started getting a burning desire to be wealthy and successful. It would become even stronger as events of the future unfolded.

Around 1983, my dad met a guy called Moni Singh. Smooth talker, settled in Los Angeles, wanting to buy handicrafts. Soon, they made plans to sell high-end carpets to the US by setting up a showroom in Beverly Hills. I would shift to the US, graduate there, and help in the showroom. Dad and his partner invested and borrowed heavily to send a large consignment on credit. Moni did rent the showroom on Wilshire Boulevard and reported the sale of a couple of carpets. Soon, his reports started becoming fewer, and when the time came for

Unwrapped Wishes

him to make the payment, he disappeared. After several attempts at contacting him, he reappeared and sent a polaroid of a window with a bullet shot. He said there had been a robbery; he was shot in the bargain and needed time to pay up. Dad's partner smelled a rat, and both rushed to the US unannounced. Lo and behold, Moni was living a king's life by selling the carpets and had gone through most of the stock. They recovered what was left and shipped it to Dad's dear friend Lute Jerstad in Portland, Oregon.

Lute Jerstad was an avid traveler and climber. He was part of the 1963 American Mount Everest Expedition and the second American to reach the summit with Barry Bishop. Jim Whittaker had become the first American to reach the summit from another route three weeks earlier. Lute was an absolute gem with quick wit and deep blue eyes. He had been introduced to Dad by a family friend, and they soon took a great liking for each other. They started working together to try to sell American products in India and vice versa. Both had a keen interest in new technologies, and he would find many new products being developed in the US for sale in India.

Lute had a friend, Jack Havens, owner of Exportech Inc., who had acquired international rights to a new coating technology – 100% Solids Polyurethane

Coatings, aka Purethane. I think this was 1984, in my second year of college. He had a coated pipe sample (which we still have) and some liquid materials. Dimple and I immediately applied the sample on the roof of the office. The stuff looked good. Both were doing Chemistry (Hons.), which seemed right up our alley. Raj had joined a Tea Estate and would come to the business after a few years. For the next few years, we did market research and wrote to and met several leading companies to sell the product. The technical manager of Exportech, a sweet old guy called David Woody, came to India and patiently explained the technology and the art of selling the product. I absorbed every word he spoke and the document he shared. Dave gave me a great insight into the know-how and American selling techniques for the product, which I would use later in life.

Our prospective customers were fascinated with the product, but unfortunately, the customs duty in India was 300%, which tossed out any chance we had of making an actual sale. We asked Jack if we could manufacture the product in India. They came up with a Coca-Cola concentrate type of proposal in which we would buy the key ingredients from them and blend them with local materials. Unfortunately, the royalty terms, including guaranteed quarterly payments, were beyond our financial capability. Finally, we had to drop the whole thing. In hindsight, it was probably for the best because the technology was ahead of its time, even in the US. Years later, when we finally started making Purethane, it was a big struggle to sell due to sheer novelty.

Dad parted ways with his partner, and things became difficult financially after the Moni Singh debacle. We had lost *everything*. We had no source of income, and all the expenses continued. Dad and Mom never let us know about the financial struggles, and we went on our merry lives as usual. Later, it became a life lesson: never burden children with your own problems. They are not equipped to handle them in the way that you are.

Unwrapped Wishes

Dimple and I had never considered taking a job, assuming we would be doing business. Raj had taken up a job in the Tea Garden and used to provide all the help he could with his starting salary. In the middle of the crisis, Mom's uncle visited one evening. I saw Mom and Dad distraught, and I wondered why. I overheard that they had no money to get him anything special to eat or drink. I walked out of the house distressed and roamed around the roads of Greater Kailash 2 for two hours, tears in my eyes. I promised myself that I would change things, come what may. I got a lifetime of motivation during those two hours. I went back home strangely calm. The starting gun had been fired, and I had taken off the block for the marathon. I went home to find everyone laughing and chatting. We had a lovely evening.

IV
Finding Our Feet

We shifted to NOIDA, a suburb of New Delhi, in 1986. We had booked an Army Welfare Housing Organization flat in Sector 29 many years ago and had started receiving pay or cancel notices. It cost us $10,000 with interest, which was a princely sum back then. We had applied for a housing loan but the application was rejected. A better-off, very close relative refused to give a loan since she would lose interest, breaking her bank fixed deposit. Fortunately, we made $3,000 just then in a trading deal to export refugee relief cookware for the UNHCR. Raj was saving everything he earned in the Tea Garden job and pitched in all he had. Somehow, we paid for the house and shifted there. At that time, NOIDA was a desolate city, but we were used to that!

Dad had started an international marketing company called IMDS (International Marketing Development Services). We had no office, so we started one in our house's 10' X 20' garage. The intervening door to the house was removed. We got it laminated and fixed four steel legs, which served as our conference table on which the boys would sit. For Dad, we got a proper table made with drawers. We made wall shelves using our carpentry tools, painted them white, and hung them. Each morning, we would eat breakfast, get ready, and walk into the garage office. There was nothing to do except to think of business

Unwrapped Wishes

ideas. Faxes were a recent entry into the market, and so were electric typewriters and basic computers. We decided to set up a small business services center. Made a project report and applied to the local bank for a loan of $3,000. It was rejected! Nothing was working out.

Dad was trying his hand at international trading. We acquired a fax machine and an electric typewriter. There was so much communication with other international traders, mostly one-man armies. We were receiving and passing on inquiries for multimillions of dollars' worth of Crude Oil, Gold, Wheat, Coal, Edible Oil, and whatnot. It was always the next deal where we would strike it rich. It never happened. We did come close once on an 800,000 MT Wheat barter trade with a US customer who did not perform.

Meanwhile, we got small orders for the export of artificial jewelry. We used to get them fabricated from the back alleys sweatshops of Old Delhi. Mom also exported traditional Indian bridal wear to an Indian store in Vancouver, Canada. She used to travel to Sadar Bazar and spend days in the dingy alleys with us, buying the stuff. We used to haul them home, put them in boxes, wrap gunny around them, sew the burlap, stencil the customer's name, and ship them overseas. We were on the job on hot summer days or freezing winter nights. We used to sell only around $20,000 in a year, but it kept our kitchen running.

Neelu and I got married in 1989 amidst all this. We had the greatest of times on a shoestring budget. We were deliriously happy just being together. Even an evening snack at a roadside food stall was a happy time. You don't need too much money to be happy; it comes from the inside. She started working in a buying house soon after we got married. It was the beginning of a long and illustrious career. Her financial contribution was invaluable in my struggling years and bought me time. She always treated me with great respect and gave encouragement; this was far more valuable than the financial support.

This went on for about four years. We were very happy but I began to wonder what I was doing with my life. I was well educated, hardworking, outgoing, and focused, and all I was doing was this basic product, minimal volume export. I had been learning the ropes of business all these years, but there was no significant result. I would have had a well-paying job if I worked in the corporate world, but I was never cut out to work under anyone. Never once crossed my mind.

One fine day in 1992, we got a fax message from David Woody. He stated that Exportech had gone into bankruptcy after Jack Havens died of cancer and asked whether we would be interested in acquiring the technology. He had spoken to Jack's widow and, given our old association, wanted to give us the first shot. We were excited!! They asked for only $10,000, and I suspect they were giving us a break. We accepted the offer on the condition it would be on an outright sale basis and would involve no royalty. We signed on the dotted line without knowing how we would arrange for the money. $10,000 was a considerable sum, like what we had paid for our house, and we had only 30 days. Somehow, we borrowed the money and bought the know-how. Game on! Finally, there was something to do that matched our education and interests.

Unwrapped Wishes

For the next few months, I poured over every page of the technology documents. The formulation was precise, and I spent a great deal of time understanding the function of each ingredient and possible sources of supply. This was much before the internet, and I had to find and consult books and directories for answers. The plant design was very poorly described, more like a child's drawing. Exportech never owned a plant and had the product toll manufactured by someone. The drawing resulted from visits to the toll manufacturer facility and was reproduced from memory!

On 19th May 1993, we incorporated Amchem Products Pvt. Ltd with Dad, Lute, Raj, Dimple and me as shareholders. It was an Indo-US Joint Venture! There was no money really to implement the project. We applied for a bank loan, giving our home as collateral. Learning from our earlier fiasco with the business center loans, we made a detailed project report with profitability projections and market prospects. The bank agreed, and things started to look up. I learned from this experience that if you want people to invest in your idea, it is not sufficient to make an emotional two-line pitch that you think you can do. You need to convince them that the homework has been done in detail and that you have a clear-cut financial plan to ensure returns and safety of their money. To every frustrated, budding entrepreneur, don't blame your lack of finances for failure to start your business. Many people are ready to invest; you need to generate confidence that you can create a profitable business by presenting a proper business plan. Trust me, try it.

We first tried to get an engineering firm to design and build the whole plant. The name that came to my mind was a large EPC contractor, Larsen & Toubro. We fixed up a meeting through a VIP connection and went along with our child's drawing. To give them credit, the guys were very nice and did not fall down their chairs laughing. Very politely, they told us that we only do projects of $25 million or more. They said your work is small and would cost less than $50,000.

We then sent the requirements to many fabricators, who all requested drawings. We realized that there was a disconnect. Although we broadly understood the process, we needed to translate it into a proper equipment design and drawing. After disappointing discussions with a few consultants, we finally got a reference of a one-person consulting firm owned by Ranadhi Banerjee. Very talented person and well versed in high vacuum technology which we needed. He was also doing secret projects for the government since he would inform and become incognito for a few weeks. We signed up the equipment design deal for about $3,000. Together, we sat for about a hundred hours converting the child's drawing to a proper design that we could fabricate. He also offered to get the core reactor manufactured through his vendors. We agreed and signed up for $15,000 with steel to be arranged by us (another learning opportunity). He wasn't in control of the vendors, and it would take them 18 months to deliver. This, too, happened after we spent hundreds of hours in their facilities pushing and prodding. In some cases, we reclaimed half-built equipment to get it finished elsewhere. Meanwhile, we also arranged for the pumps, heating, cooling equipment, and the like from other sources.

Unwrapped Wishes

The three of us were always very mechanically inclined, especially Dimple. Since childhood, we have constantly tinkered with making all kinds of contraptions. My talent is to grasp a concept and convert that into reality. Raj is the one who brings order to the chaos. Getting the building designed and made and the equipment fabricated, erected, and commissioned was such a learning experience. During those years, we learned so much about process plants, heating, cooling, power, electricity, control panels, motors, ASME codes, piping, flanges, welding, and vacuum. We bought books on plant engineering and researched in detail. Practically, we did everything either by our own hands or sitting on the heads of the workers. We even hung from ropes from the roof and welded the vessel support structures. Later, when the plant was ready, we learned about coating application, sandblasting, and airless spraying. First, by reading about them in detail and then by doing them by our owns hands. Our first commercial job was on the roof of an apartment building owned by Raj's friend, where Raj did the entire spray himself! Things came naturally to us, although we dedicated much time and effort. This would play a significant role in the future as we would remain leagues ahead of everyone in technology.

Domain knowledge is the single biggest differentiator for success. General education, school, and college set you up to receive and build domain knowledge. Domain knowledge is not restricted to occupations that require a degree but also trade skills. The latter will become even more critical as AI takes away many of the former's jobs.

After graduating from college, I learned a bit about theoretical chemistry and some practical laboratory work. However, I knew nothing about real-world chemical industry skills, not even how to make a paint can. I learned that on the job—an industry internship in real life!

Many people consider graduation to be the end of education. It is only the beginning. Also, the importance of reputed education institutes is highly overrated. What matters is the quality of education you received, which in many parts depends upon the interest you paid during that time. We are obsessed with getting astronomical scores to get into a good institute, primarily because of their shortage. This compels us to put in excessive hours of studying at the cost of learning other life skills or even just enjoying the growing up years playing sports, hobbies, traveling, or spending time with friends.

Coming back to domain knowledge. I once read a remarkable passage on how hundreds of companies comprising thousands of employees are required to build a modern jetliner. Human achievement has been possible mainly due to the collaboration of billions of people. Each person contributes their domain knowledge. There are about 8 billion people in the world competing for a living. You are not valued enough if you have nothing significant to contribute. The higher the domain knowledge, the higher the return. That's why focusing on a specific field in life is so important, as well as building up domain knowledge over the years by learning all you can.

By December 1995, the plant was ready. We had chosen a 1000-litre reactor instead of the 4000-litre design used by Exportech. We did not anticipate demand to justify the larger size, and we could greatly economize on costs. The decision was correct for some years, but when demand suddenly shot up, we had a very tough time keeping up. During our expansion phase, we made sure this did not happen, and our next plant was twice what we anticipated.

The plant performed flawlessly, and the quality was first-rate. However, the batch cycle was too long since some of the ancillary equipment was under capacity. It took us 18-20 hours to make a batch, which meant staying up all night to finish. We used to make the batches ourselves and had only three workers handling the material. Since we had negligible sales, it did not matter how long the batch took.

We had a staff of zero, so we used to do everything ourselves: purchasing, manufacturing, labeling the drums, invoicing, dispatching, accounts, banking, marketing, etc. It was a great learning experience for us as we got to know the intricacies of each function and build domain knowledge. We had much free time to learn more things like coating applications. Much time was spent reading books and experimenting to develop the knowledge pool. This is critical to driving any business since you can pass this on to your organization and employees as the company grows.

Doing everything yourself has its downside. While you gain deep business knowledge, you start getting used to doing all the work yourself. It becomes challenging to let go and delegate the work to staff. The usual justifications of 'no one can do the job like I do' or 'I'm saving so much salary cost' come up. I firmly believe no one can perform and produce results like the founders. However, the workload starts to become unmanageable. At the right moment, the entrepreneur needs to start setting up the organization and focus on things he should be doing rather than on mundane tasks. The exact moment will depend upon each business and anticipated cash flow, but I would rather it be sooner. In our case, it was very late, detrimental to the company's growth. We were the market's most outstanding performers for many years but smaller than we ought to be. It was just not humanely possible for us to do more work.

The founder's mode of running a business is not fully understood. Professional managers often do not produce the same result as the founder, and scaling up by hiring good people often does not work as anticipated. It could be that professional managers are hyping up their skills, capabilities, or even actual past performance. It could be that their motivation and zeal are not on par with the founders. We are struggling with the answer to these questions and hope to find a solution in the coming years.

Numerous start-ups nowadays quickly ramp up operations without a profitable business model or even a cash flow projection. To me, this is a strange way of doing business, enabled only by easy venture capital money. Many of them will fall by the wayside, and their valuations will disappear into thin air. Everyone loses except the professional job jumpers hired by desperate companies at great cost during the rush to scale up.

V
Going To Market

In early 1996, we were ready and itching to sell. I had already done a lot of market research and had identified prospective customers. The areas where Purethane had been successful in the US, Middle East, and Japan were obviously the first choice, municipal wastewater being the first on the list. We visited various municipal authorities and saw their operating water and sewage treatment plants. The Okhla sewage treatment plant chief engineer had proudly kept a few glasses of treated wastewater and claimed it was good enough to drink. He went ahead and gulped it down and offered me one. I don't remember how I managed to get out of that one, but it was probably a stellar excuse.

Corrosion was a significant issue, and current products were not working well. That was a considerable opportunity right away! Unfortunately, they had very low budgets and were used to only basic coatings such as Coal Tar Enamel. Even though they liked the product and wanted to buy it, it was way beyond their budget by a factor of three. Technology upgradation was a slow process back then, especially with the government departments. It would have been impossible for them to justify the cost, even if it meant a tenfold increase in the service life. Two decades later, they would adopt these technologies but were not ready back then. They would have saved much more by using the coating and preventing early failure of their infrastructure.

After a few months, I realized the situation was also true in other areas. It was a notoriously price-sensitive market, and customers would gag at the initial cost even though it would save considerable sums in the long run. I remember a meeting in Mumbai with one of the largest coating applicators in India. This Parsi gentleman condescendingly agreed to see me. He heard me leaning backward in his plush executive chair and pronounced, "No one will ever buy this." Although I was seething, I imagined he had leaned too far back and flipped over! With that happy image, I smiled, told him, "Let's see," and walked out.

I was getting the same reaction from everyone I was meeting. People who did not balk at the price offered the usual excuses: Give us a track record in India, who else is using it, and so on. The excellent international track record was not enough. Despite tons of data about the performance, these were just timid tactics of playing safe and not being the first to use. The dream of quick sales soured very quickly. It was very disheartening, to say the least.

We needed to change track and rethink the approach completely. We needed to encourage a mindset that looks at what works in the long term, protects assets far more valuable than the cost of coating, and has the lowest cost per annum. Of course, they would also need to have the money to afford this in the first place. The latter was easier to identify; customers in the Oil and Gas sector and Power did have the money. Convincing them was a tremendous task, though.

For the next few years, I traveled extensively to meet potential customers. Luckily, quite a few had headquarters in NOIDA, including the Indian Oil - Pipeline Division, Projects and Development India PDIL, and National Thermal Power Corp. NTPC, so it was more affordable, and I could visit them more often.

Unwrapped Wishes

I also took trips to Pune, Mumbai, Bangalore, Chennai, Hyderabad, Kolkata and back home. The round trip would remove the cost of the return flights, except the last one. I would stay in budget hotels and travel by auto-rickshaws between meetings. The travel was challenging since I tried to squeeze out the most in a minimal amount of time. I would not take any breaks between the sessions and would meet as many people as possible in a day. The whole purpose was to return home as quickly as possible to my family and my darling little boys Sachit and Aryan. I would time the trips Monday to Friday so I would be back home for the weekend.

I shouldn't complain about the trips because I thoroughly enjoyed the experience of meeting and interacting with people at senior levels of large corporations. Learning how the corporate world and industry functioned widened my horizons considerably. It also taught me that there are all types of people in the corporate world: happy, irritated, angry, disinterested, insulting, and enthusiastic, and all need to be handled differently. I once met a senior project manager at a power company who declared that all our current products work perfectly and we do not need anything new. Instead of arguing, I politely said, well, in that case, I have no business wasting your time, thanked him, and left.

Six months later, we were sitting together, finalizing a major pipe project with enthusiasm. The latter deal would not have happened had I shown my irritation and anger at his statement.

During this time, I must have met well over two hundred people nationwide in about four dozen companies and government departments. The response remained the same; most liked the product, but no one wanted to be the first in the industry. I realized that the efforts were getting spread too thin, and I made return visits to customers after a long period. I reflected on the people who were most ready to bell the cat. There were only two on the list. I put the more extensive list on hold for a while and focussed only on these two people. Providing them vast amounts of technical data, product comparative, life cycle analysis, international references, and overseas customer feedback. Our sales literature and communication quality were of international standard, having learned much from David Woody.

I used to make so many visits to NTPC, which was only about 3 miles away from our plant. Every possible department, every concerned person. Many in the company started thinking I worked there. Talking endlessly about how their project could benefit from the technology. Just then, they started working on a project which would use seawater for cooling for the first time. Obviously, corrosion was a significant concern. They had done a lot of research on similar international projects. They realized that conventional corrosion protection mechanisms would not suffice. Some brilliant engineers were working there, and the whole building was buzzed with activity. Their go-to guy for technical decisions was Manik Chatterjee. He immediately realized that Purethane was a possible answer. Fortunately, we had a lot of data from Exportech and their Japanese licensee, Mitsui. For over a decade, Mitsui successfully applied the coating to seawater-cooled power stations in Japan. That gave them confidence.

NTPC asked us to make a presentation. About a hundred engineers and top brass were to attend in their auditorium. While I was very confident in small meetings, I had a big phobia of addressing big groups back then. Probably went back to my childhood when I sang a wholly miserable and incoherent song at one of the kid's birthday parties. As the date for the presentation approached, I became more and more anxious. I prayed for time to fast forward beyond the date. Canceling would have effectively put an end to our proposal. In the morning, I felt sick to my stomach but went anyway. Had never backed off from a situation. Just before the presentation, I felt like throwing up, so I went to the nearest toilet and did just that. Now that there was nothing to empty in front of the audience, I returned and did the presentation. Even ended up cracking a few jokes. Later, after giving many of these, I became very comfortable and gave hundreds with complete ease. Raj and Dimple had arranged a live spray in front of the building. Everyone trooped to the site and saw the spray. Nothing to beat seeing the product in real life. Everything went off flawlessly.

After the live demo, we had a small meeting in the Executive Director's office. They formally decided to specify products for two areas, Seawater Cooling Towers and pipelines. A bunch of guys in their early thirties had successfully pitched a high-technology solution to India's most significant power company for a billion-dollar project. Dad's presence and contribution to the meeting went a long way in giving them confidence.

Around this time, Indian Oil sought a candidate coating for Buried LPG Tanks. PDIL handled the consultancy, and Dr. MB Mishra was the technical lead. We shared all the technical data and test reports provided by Exportech for similar applications, and he saw merit in the product and ended up specifying it for the application.

We and the entire industry will remain forever indebted to these two gentlemen, Manik Chatterjee from NTPC and Dr. MB Mishra from PDIL, for having the courage to look beyond and reach out into the future.

I have always been honest and transparent in my approach to the customers, resulting in them trusting me fully. Never be too clever and misuse the trust your customers place in you. Many people think a marketing person is a slick willy, someone with the gift of the gab. He will hypnotize you with his words and make you buy things that you don't need. Nothing can be further from the truth! The best marketing person patiently listens to the customer, identifies his pain points, and offers a solution to meet his needs. Should know his subject thoroughly. Anything else is pure deceit.

Over the next two decades, Amchem single-handedly changed the industry by making all the firsts: the first new cross-country pipeline, pipeline rehabilitation, sewage treatment plants, ductile iron pipe, and water pipelines. In each sector, the specifications of the market leader were copied by others in the field, and this product became the de facto standard in many industries.

I never induced any of these people, and most never asked. I detested the ones who asked and walked away. In my mind, they were just scum of the earth.

The success in converting the market was not just due to selling but by performing very solidly in the application at the site, handled by Raj and Dimple in highly challenging conditions. I will cover many of these in the following few chapters. No competitor making 100% Solids Polyurethane Coatings ever made any inroads into newer markets. They ate what we grew by offering diluted, low-cost me-too products applied by inexperienced and low-price applicators. We lost a lot of business to these companies because many contractors did not regard quality and customers' well-being and just wanted a slight extra profit. We saw examples of these highly poor-quality works and were horrified. The lowest bidder system is a very retrograde step. Quality is never evaluated properly; only questionable documents are filed in compliance with specifications. Then, it is a free-for-all in execution, supported by 'friendly' inspectors.

Selling through 'contacts and connections' is a very poor idea. We, too, tried this route in the initial period. My uncle was very influential in political circles. We immediately thought of asking him to introduce us to large corporations. He agreed, and I met him in Mumbai for a sales trip I will never forget. He fixed an appointment with two of the most significant industrial houses in the country, not with the management but with the owners. We were both given a very warm welcome. For the first meeting, the owner arrived on top of the building in his private chopper and sat for a 30-minute discussion over tea. We were asked to continue the discussions in the board meeting, which had been previously scheduled.

So, I sat next to him as he was conducting the meeting. He spent his time talking to the board and me on the side. I heard them casually talk about buying multiple $100 million oil rigs as they were some new cars they were buying. He was a brilliant guy, very polite, and he seemed impressed by the product and discussed various areas in his operations that could benefit from it. Afterward, he asked one of his directors to refer us to heads of divisions. I left the building feeling lightheaded. What a fantastic start. The volumes would be huge. Later, when we contacted the division heads, they referred me to the GMs, the Managers, etc. Finally, I reached the people I had spoken to earlier! Looking back, they were probably used to this stuff and were not saying no to the big boss. In fact, the lower rungs resented that I had skydived from the top.

The experience with the other industrial house, which was even more significant, was identical. But to his credit, the owner told me, "I think you have a good product. You don't need the help of all these people. Just go to the market and sell. Don't bother with all these so-called contacts."

Nothing came of the grand Mumbai trip. Many years later, we sold products to both companies the usual way: by meeting the concerned persons, offering, discussing, and negotiating—the way it should be done.

Sometimes, you meet very poor people and end up reacting very badly. One LPG tank fabrication customer invited us over the phone after discussing and freezing the price and the terms and conditions. It was only a formality of signing the contract. Raj and I took the train, stayed overnight, and drove an hour to the outskirts for the meeting. The waiting lasted over two hours, and I realized something was wrong. Finally, we were informed that the meeting would not occur, and we had to return home. I just blew my top. In the middle of their office, I started screaming at the top of my voice about how unprofessional the company was and what a miserable bunch they were. Raj had to restrain me from barging into the concerned person's office and creating a scene. We found out later that a competing company with unusual connections with one of the executive directors had intervened and made that happen. The owner had died, and his young son was running the show. He was probably brow beaten by the wily fox.

A similar situation happened in Mumbai. I introduced the fabricator of LPG tanks to the end customer, and he secured a $25 Million contract. He invited me to sign the coating contract in Mumbai, made me wait the whole day, and called me in for the meeting just before leaving for the airport in the evening. He told me he would need more time to decide and asked for a deep discount. Disgusted, I walked away amazed at the morals of people. You will meet people of every kind in this world. Pathetic.

Fortunately, there are good people, too! In a quirk of fate, I introduced another fabricator of LPG tanks to a prospective customer, Deepak Fertilizers. The fabrication company was Fabtech Projects, based out of Pune, and the owner was BA Rupnar. He was a real dynamo. The moment we spoke on the phone, he called his team in, discussed the lead, and, in an hour, was off to Mumbai to meet the customer. By the end of the day, he had closed the deal! In the evening, he called me and gave me the good news. He told me that Fabtech would buy coatings only from Amchem for as long as he lived. He was true to his word and never negotiated with me. Our phone calls were legendary. He was hard-pressed for time, and the calls would last only about 20 seconds. How are you doing, Mr. Mann? Long time no see; what price should I put on the PO? OK, done. He was one of the most energetic and dynamic people I ever met. He took his company from about $2 Million in turnover to over

$400 Million in about a decade. Unfortunately, he died of a heart attack at a relatively young age.

One of the biggest mistakes entrepreneurs make is underestimating the time it will take to generate a positive cash flow and a profit. Whatever your projection said, add at least two or three years to that and be ready with the working capital for that period. So many new and promising businesses close during this phase. We almost did several times. Although the product had been specified in a few places, those projects were some years away, and we would have revenue much later. We had run out of cash and needed more urgently. It would come from an unexpected source.

VI
The Russian Adventure

We were always savvy with technology. In early 1997, our website was up and running within about a year of the Internet becoming live in India. Dimple had designed and set up the website. We had nothing much to contribute by way of our own work, so we relied on Exportech data and pictures. The Internet gave excellent visibility to smaller companies that did not have the budget for traditional advertising.

Around September 1997, out of the blue, we got an email from FAB GmbH Germany asking if we could do a pipe coating job in Uzbekistan. A 40" Dia, 1-inch wall thickness, 1-mile long Gas Pipeline section for Gazprom Russia will be installed via horizontal directional drilling (HDD) under the Nukus River by a Dutch company, NACAP. At that time, it was the largest HDD project in the world. Polyurethanes were suitable for this work since they could withstand the pull operation without damage. Of course, we would do it! They were in a hurry since they had to deliver the gas to the region before the onset of the winter, and only this section remained. We were informed that the ambient temperature would be around $10^\circ C$, which was manageable. The pipes were scheduled to be delivered by train from Germany in about 3 weeks, and we had to airlift the coating materials and equipment.

Shomendra Mann

We airfreighted the primer from Mitsui Japan directly to Tashkent, and our materials and spray equipment were from India. The schedule was so rushed that our coating drums were still hot off the reactor when we sent them to the airport! The three of us and our only three workers flew to Tashkent to do the application, which would take about 2 weeks. Our factory was closed for this duration. Arrival was a bit of a shock; heavily armed military personnel were on the runway. It was cold, around -5^oC, although it was early in the morning. We were taken to the Gazprom office for an initial meeting before catching our next flight to Nukus. It was a very friendly, grand lunch which involved a lot of, what else, neat Vodka! Raj wasn't much of a drinker and ended up sick. The hotel in Nukus was basically an old, abandoned residential building with minimal facilities. The rooms were not even heated.

As it turned out, the pipes were delayed by three weeks. In the interim, we had nothing to do except walk around Nukus, which seemed strangely abandoned with dozens of huge, empty buildings. There were very few people to be seen around. The ones who spotted us would scream 'Raj Kapoor' and rush to meet us since they were fond of Indian movies. It also started becoming extremely cold, with subzero temperatures at night! We would keep our laundry out, and it would be frozen stiff. Shifting it inside did not help much, as the room radiator was broken.

Our bodies started to become low on energy, and we shivered constantly. I bought some vodka bottles and would have a shot whenever it became too cold, but we were getting sick of it. The first day, we had seen the cow being cut Hilal and bleating to death just beyond the window. So, we had been opting for bread and vegetables and not eating the animal meat broth in the dining hall. Our bodies started to tell us we need animal fat to survive! We soon started eating it, and things improved. One afternoon, we decided it would be impossible to carry on like this and that we needed to buy warmer clothes. We had packed only for 10^oC. The only place to buy something warm was the roadside daily market, and we went there. It was -10^oC with powerful winds. We bought boots, gloves, thermals, and jackets. Before I could wear them, the cold had already done the trick. I got hypothermia and started shivering uncontrollably. I rushed back to the room, put on my clothes, was given two hot coffees, and went under three layers of the quilt. After about half an hour, I stopped shivering and returned to normal. It was a close shave.

Teams of many nationalities were doing the project, including Uzbeks, Russians, Germans, and Dutch. We were assigned an interpreter of Ukrainian origin, a friendly, easy-going older man named Peter, who spoke Russian and English.

The guy in charge of the Gazprom team was a tough old hard hat called Sidorov (in pic). We heard rumors that he was connected to the KGB; he looked and behaved like that. We were also assigned an escort for unknown reasons, a tough, late twenties local guy named Bhaktiyar. Again, the rumor was that he was related to the mafia. He was a very outgoing fellow, and we got along very well. One day though, he had an argument with a waiter over some imagined affront, and the next day, the waiter was found dead with his throat slit. It must be just a coincidence. There was a lot of tension in the project camp due

to the delay. Apparently, the minister had promised the region's people that gas would be available before the onset of the winter, and the project just had to be finished. The site in charge of the EPC, FAB, was found naked beside the river one morning. Probably tried to kill himself or was thrown inside. No one told us what had happened, but he quickly left for home the same day. His replacement, Uwe, was a big, hulky German. Very friendly but tough, nonetheless. He knew how to withstand the pressure from the Russian team. Super guy.

The pipes finally arrived on site and the Uzbek team started making the HDD crossing string. The Dutch team was very friendly and chilled out. They had installed speakers on masts, which would play fantastic music while they worked drilling the 1 mile-long hole under the river. A super, heated camper was parked on site, where they used to relax and have food and beer. We were invited many times to join in. At times, it went to -20^oC, and getting inside the warm camper was such a big relief. It seemed we would die if we stood outside any longer. Our breath would freeze on our mustaches. For fun, we would remove one glove to see how quickly the skin started to freeze.

Unwrapped Wishes

We started going to the site to prepare for the coating. It was about an hour's drive in big army-type trucks through complete wilderness. On one side of the river was the Dutch crew digging the hole, and on the other was the pipe being welded together by local Uzbeks. We had to cross the river on small rubber dinghies to reach the other side. The Amu Darya had crystal clear water. After about three days, the temperatures plummeted, and the river suddenly froze overnight. We then used to walk across the ice, which was dangerous. I checked with Bhaktiyar to see whether it was safe to walk across. Sure, he replied. We check the depth of the ice by throwing rocks and listening to the sound. Comes naturally to us, he says. On the third day, we were walking across the street as usual, with the guys in front throwing rocks onto the ice. Suddenly, the ice beneath me broke, and I went down into the fast-flowing river. Luckily at that point, the water was only waist deep, and I wasn't sucked underneath and swept away. You wouldn't be reading this book if this happened just a few feet ahead. I was taken out and let out the loudest and vilest string of Hindi expletives ever heard in Uzbekistan on the people in charge and their rock-throwing and listening skills. Had to remove my clothes and sit naked in front of a fire they lit up in my honor. After this episode, they got wooden planks and nailed them to each other to make a narrow walkway.

We finally started the coating application process. Set up the equipment in a covered truck with a compressor in tow. The only issue was the freezing temperatures. In the morning, all the equipment was frozen. The Russians were used to this and lit small fires under the trucks and compressors to warm them enough to start. We could not do the same to our Graco spray equipment! We used to start the drum heaters and heat the materials. Air heaters warmed up the rest of the equipment. The air hoses became so brittle that they would break if twisted. I used to operate the machinery inside the truck; Dimple and Raj were outside overseeing the spray. One crew member used to manage the manifold, and one spray operator was on each side of the pipe. We were ready. But the pipe wasn't.

We landed at the site each morning with an inch-thick layer of ice on top of the pipe. The contractor could not blast clean, and we could not spray on ice. We had repeated brainstorming sessions with Gazprom, FAB, and the blasting contractor on how to heat the pipe enough to melt the ice and warm it up to $5°C$. Remember, this was in the middle of nowhere with no equipment or significant energy source for a hundred miles. We installed air heaters next to the pipe and turned them on. Nothing. All the warm air used to escape into the blue sky. Then they got an old semicircular army-type steel shed, put it over a section of the pipe using cranes, and turned on the heater again. Zilch, Nada. The sheer heat required was way beyond the capability of the air heaters. Any back envelope calculations would have shown that.

We had reached a stalemate, and tempers were flying high. The Dutch team furiously dug away the underground hole and pumped it with bentonite to

prevent collapse. They would be ready soon and could not assure that the hole would remain for long after finishing. I concluded nothing could be done until the weather cleared, which meant returning in the spring. We went to Sidorov and proposed this option, and the Dutch team also concurred. He would not have any of this. In no uncertain terms, he said that we all would go back once the job was over. Our passports were taken away for visa renewal since the original execution period had elapsed. We would only see them once the project was over. Disappointed and homesick, I had lost a little nerve and felt guilty about broaching the subject with the Dutch and Sidorov. Raj kept steadfast and strong.

We would go to the site each day and look for a solution. Other crews were working, welding the pipe into a string and testing. We would return to the camp each evening, tired and full of site dust. After a bath, all the crew would get together for drinks and dinner with traditional Uzbek and Russian dance, just like what we saw in the movie Titanic years later. That part was so much fun.

Unwrapped Wishes

We were also entirely cut off from our folks back home. FAB had only one satellite phone with a connected fax. It was horribly expensive, and every user had to pay to send and receive messages. We managed to exchange notes once or twice a week at home. We had informed them about the hopeless situation at the site and our travails. It was natural for them to be highly anxious about our well-being. Neelu was expecting our second child, Aryan, who was due in two weeks. I longed to be back home in time. Neelu told me later that Sachit insisted during my absence that he would not allow me to go anywhere again because he had forgotten my face.

Shortly after, Sidorov called us for a meeting. They had finally arrived at an ingenious solution! A runway ice-melting equipment had been located at Nukus airport. This was an MIG-15 jet engine that was fixed to the back of a kerosene tanker. The engine was fired, and the exhaust would generate enormous amounts of heat to melt the ice off runways. The equipment was removed from the airport, parked at the edge of the pipe with exhaust going inside, and turned on. The entire 1-mile length was hot in 30 minutes. Game on! We had to keep contact thermometers where we sprayed to ensure the surface did not overheat. We also kept tabs on the operators via walkie-talkies.

We went on overdrive to finish the project. Didn't even take lunch breaks. We bought a lot of Snicker bars, which we would keep in our overalls and pop in while working.

The moment the last pipe was coated, I wanted to rush back. I think I took the last flight back home the next day and reached just days before Aryan was born on 21 December 1997. Raj, Dimple, and the crew stayed to see the pipe being pulled through on 16 December, pack up, and send back the equipment. As soon as the pipe was pulled through, it started snowing, which meant the end of operations. The coating performed well and withstood the heavy abrasion of being pulled through a mile-long hole. The steel pull head attached to the front end came out bright and shiny with all the abrasion, but the adjacent coating was fully intact.

The whole project was a great success, and there was a lot of bonhomie and bonding among everyone who took part. Sidorov finally cracked a big smile, with much laughter and celebration. Senior officials of Gazprom and the minister came to congratulate and cheer everyone on the project's timely completion. To this day, I remember the whole project vividly. I remember the sheer hard

Unwrapped Wishes

work and determination everyone involved showed under highly challenging conditions. When the going gets tough, the tough get going.

Although we had initially asked for around $85,000, we renegotiated towards the end. We got almost $165,000 and a thank-you from the customer. This money would see us through for about two more years.

VII
THE EQUIPMENT WORKED!

Immediately after returning from the Russian adventure, we did two small waterproofing works, one for a friend making a shopping mall (SAB in Sector 18) and one for the rooftop garden of my uncle's home. Although Purethane wasn't initially targeted at waterproofing work, the outstanding performance made us consider introducing a roller-applied variant, Drythane, about 25 years later. We had dug up a small portion of the rooftop lawn after about 20 years and found that the coating was in pristine shape. It had given complete sealing for this period and continues to do so.

Lute sadly passed away on 31 October 1998 after a massive heart attack on a trip to the Everest base camp with his grandson Marshall. It was a shocking and sad time for us. He was buried on the land he loved the most, the Himalayas. Lute was convinced that Amchem would be a grand success and would tell everyone how talented we three were. He was sorely missed, and it was unfortunate that he could not see our success in later years.

Unwrapped Wishes

For the next two years, we did not do physical sales and were busy concept selling across industry segments. We did demonstration projects for pipeline rehabilitation for Indian Oil, a new pipeline simulator for the Gas Authority of India, and a small sewage pipelining project for the Delhi Jal Board. These were just proof-of-concept works and did not contribute much to sales. However, each was a great learning opportunity in application.

For the Jal Board project, we designed and developed automated lining tools that cost us more than the total sales revenue. We learned about high-quality blast cleaning, and Amchem used Granulated Copper Slag for the first time in India. Till this time, the industry had been using sand for blast cleaning, which generated hazardous dust and transferred contaminants to the surface. We acquired many specialized coating application books and subscribed to a coatings magazine from the US called The Journal of Protective Coatings and Linings (JPCL), which opened our horizons to the best practices of surface preparation and coating application in America. We studied these in-depth and emulated them in our own operations.

In late 2000, we got a call from Dr. Mishra from Projects Development India PDIL. Bharat Petroleum Corp BPCL Haldia wanted to install a petroleum pipeline from the jetty to their terminal. The pipes had already been procured and were lying in stock at the site, and they could not send them back to a coating plant. There were about 3 miles of 16" and 24" pipeline each, and the work had to be done urgently, with a completion period of 3 months from the date of order. Could we do it? Never ask the three musketeers this question; the answer will always be **YES**. We signed the contract with the successful bidder, Expo Gas Mumbai, and the timer was started.

Some back envelope calculations showed that the blast cleaning capacity required was about $100m^2$ per hour. Blast cleaning is the process where abrasive particles are projected at high velocity using compressed air onto a rusted steel surface to clean it and produce a sandpaper-like roughness for bonding. This was 20 times the capability of our standard 200 kg portable blaster, which would blast for 10 minutes and then take 10 minutes to refill. It could only use an 8 mm nozzle, achieving only $10m^2$ per hour when working non-stop. Something needed to be done urgently. Also, we wanted the coating to be perfectly even, with minimal overspray. It could not be hand-sprayed. That would be an old-fashioned way of doing things, something against our grain. We needed to get to the drawing board, design, build, and deliver the equipment in about 8 weeks.

We had been ogling and salivating at the bulk blasting equipment in the US for some years. I even had happy dreams of these at night. They could take multiple nozzles of up to ½ inch, hold up to 5,000 kgs of abrasive, and blast continuously for hours. It would beautifully match our requirements. Unfortunately, they were 8,000 miles, $30,000, and 5 months away. Similarly, their pipe-spinning units were super. They had a track alongside on which a four-wheel cart could travel with blast nozzles or spray tips. The system would be automated with variable-speed drives, and we would get excellent quality. If wishes were horses....

Pushed to the wall, we arrived at an audacious plan. What if we fabricate the equipment in India and get the key components by air from the US? The whole question was, would the damn thing work? I recalled our experience with the child drawings of the manufacturing plant and decided to go for it. We had no choice in any case.

Enter Sudesh Jha, owner of my neighboring factory, who manufactures various bespoke equipment. He is a brilliant guy; from then on, he has been friends forever. People who have started from scratch and gone on to build something have a great respect for each other, which he and I have shared. Later, he built a lot of equipment for us, including our next plant. I walked across the road to his factory hesitantly and described what we wanted to do. He was a true entrepreneur, ready for anything. We spoke for hours, looking at pictures of the equipment and trying to decipher them. He said, you provide all the process design, technology, and parts, and I will fabricate the thing. Should work, with the operative word being should. He was confident about the pipe rollers, but we need to provide the inputs for everything else as he didn't have any experience.

I went back to the factory and discussed it with Dimple at length. Seemed like something we could do. Promptly, I got on my computer and started sketching the broad outlines of the equipment and calculating outputs and capacities, air consumption, and such. So far, so good. We then contacted blast cleaning valves, hoses, and parts manufacturers and started placing orders for air shipments. Sudesh converted my designs (I won't use the child word) to drawings. He had such a skill for designing. During a discussion, he would take out a paper and pen and start drawing the part based on his knowledge of materials and engineering. Based on what I knew about the process, I would intervene, saying we need to change this and that. We burned the midnight oil, getting the equipment ready. Ratios, speeds, and rotation were calculated several times, and suitable gearboxes, motors, and drives were bought from different vendors around the country and express-delivered. Some specialized parts, such as automation electrical controls, polyurethane spinning wheels, and such, were designed by us and built by vendors we had located. The 4 metric tonne pipe had to be spun at 20 RPM and would need a very sturdy rolling wheel. We found an excellent source in NOIDA, a Muvtons company, who designed and built them for us.

Looking back, what we created in 8 weeks would have taken companies a couple of years to develop. Nothing like timeline pressure to achieve results. Sudesh, Dimple, and I made an excellent equipment team. Together we achieved something that each of us alone would not have been able to do separately. When two or more people work together with full dedication to a task and have complete respect for each other's contribution, what you create, to borrow Napoleon Hill's words, is a mastermind. The mastermind can achieve amazing things. More on this later.

We used to work very late into the night. When the time came to dispatch, we had worked for 48 hours continuously and finally crashed out at dawn on the office floor after the last equipment trucks left. Couldn't even make it home. We had finally built a huge 10,000 Kgs bulk unit with three ½ inch nozzles designed for non-stop blasting the whole day! It was probably the first of its kind ever, and it needed an entire truck to transport to the site. Looking at it gave me goosebumps. We painted all the equipment white with big AMCHEM logos in green, our company color. There was no time or place to test the equipment.

Raj and Dimple went to the site while I looked after the plant. They set up all the equipment and arranged all the logistics and consumables. We hired two large compressors of 450 cfm each from Kolkata, hydra cranes locally, and about 300 MT of copper slag from Hindustan Copper, Ghatshila. We got a taste of the notorious unions at the site. They would not even let us unload the trucks unless we hired their people. We learned that hiring was a euphemism for paying people to sit around and not work. There was a fixed ratio of outside workers to the number of people we would have to hire. Luckily, most operations were automated, so we did not have to pay too much additional wages.

Site blast cleaning and coating work is challenging, especially when done by hand. The blasting hoses are very heavy, and the air pressure is about 125 lbs inside, making them very difficult to hold and maneuver. The abrasive exits from the nozzles at close to the speed of sound, so letting go accidentally is not an option. Blowing away fingers or facial parts in seconds is always on the cards. Hence, you must wear heavy protective gear, including leather-covered body suits. In hot weather, up to $45°C$, you sweat like a pig inside and quickly lose a lot of water. You need extremely tough workers to do the work.

Luckily, we had very hardy Nepali workers for the coating work. Amazingly, they would work 8 hours non-stop with just a break for lunch and some tea. Their lunches were legendary. Each person would eat 10 or more thick rotis (breads) with lentils and vegetables, about the same as a family in the city would eat. Since its inception, Amchem has arranged all the food for site workers, with hot lunches from a kitchen we set up. The food was excellent, and we often ate together. The first Nepali workers were referred by house help. In time, we adopted complete villages where Amchem employed every suitable person. Most worked their peak working age at Amchem and became legends in the company, Buddhi Bahadur, Bal Bahadur, and Rattan, to name some of these great guys. On this job, though, most operations were automated. However, there was still a lot of work, such as drying, sieving, loading the 300 MT of abrasive, and removing the used waste.

Anyway, D-Day arrived when we had to start the work. A big team from BPCL assembled for the Puja and inauguration. Amitrajit Bhattacharya, the local BPCL head, did the Puja, broke the coconut on the equipment, and said let's start. The first pipe was on the roller, waiting for blast cleaning. About a hundred eyes are watching. I was on the phone live, holding my breath. Dimple pressed the start button on the controls. There was a deafening banshee noise but nothing else! We freaked out. What the hell did we design and make? There was total panic inside but calm outside.

Dimple told them to wait a few minutes while he checked what was wrong. Quickly, he found out an NC air valve had been fitted in reverse by mistake. He removed and placed it correctly, but we were still unsure. We had never seen it working. The button was pressed again. The nozzles kicked in and started the most high-power site blast cleaning ever seen in India.

The pipes were rusty from outdoor storage, but the blast cleaning was like a hot knife on butter. Jaws dropped as everyone saw the fantastic speed of blasting and the bright steel emerge. Three 12 mm nozzles blasting together at 125 Psi finished each 12-metre pipe in minutes. The speed was 40% faster than we had calculated, and abrasive consumption was half the planning. Wow. We learned later that the Kolkata-based Indian representative of our German competitor was also hiding in the crowd. He saw the operations, was blown away, went back, and gave up the agency, realizing they could not stand up to Amchem.

The coating was equally impressive. Beautifully smooth finish and was exceptionally even due to automation. The variation in thickness was less than 100 microns, about the width of two human hairs. All the equipment worked beautifully. We went ahead and finished the pipe much ahead of schedule. A couple of days into the work, I could not resist and wanted tp see the work with my own eyes. It was amazing how everything came together. That's why I love science and technology. You can calculate, design, build and run. And will get results, no ifs, buts, or wishes. The only belief you need is in your own self.

Once the main pipe sections were over, we shifted the spray equipment to the installation site for the weld joint coating. We put our baby blasting unit on the truck, together with the spray equipment, and towed a smaller compressor that we owned. One spray operator was on either side of the pipe, and the truck moved quickly to the next joint as soon as the first one was over in minutes. We could coat a hundred joints per day this way, something unheard of in the industry. It was a grand success and a case study on how an onsite pipe coating project should be done.

At that time, we were excited about how this could be replicated on different sites nationwide. As it turned out, except for Amchem, everyone did a very shoddy job onsite. The highest technology coating in the world was being applied like ordinary house paint. We saw projects where the coating was applied with either a perfunctory blast or sometimes even without blast cleaning by completely untrained crews using makeshift equipment. There was no pride in the quality of work, only ignorance, lack of ethics, or knowledge, just the desire to make a quick buck. There was corner-cutting on every aspect, and the inspection teams were turning a blind eye for reasons best known to them. Most jobs were a complete disaster, and polyurethanes and all other coatings were given a bad name. This led to a catastrophic coating failure with plant shutdowns in many situations.

We had to go around the industry, begging customers to stop site coating work and get the job done in coating plants instead, wherever possible. In time, this would mean distancing ourselves from site coating and moving on to plant coating for pipes. More on this later.

VIII
To Climb a Mountain

While Raj and Dimple were at the Haldia site, I was busy trying to close a cooling tower project. NTPC specified the product for Seawater Pipelines and Cooling Towers for their Simadhri Project some years ago. Amchem had sold the concept to NTPC, the only company producing a proven product, and would have been a logical choice for the project. But there were wheels behind wheels. NTPC had a system where sub-vendors for each package needed to be given approval. The EPC contractor for the Make Up Water package, Navayuga Engineering Company NEC, was keen for us to do the job. We gave them our technical and commercial offers and assumed it would get through. It was about 200,000 square meters of 2.00 mm thick coating. The pipes were to be built by PSL in Vizag, close to the project site. PSL was a giant in pipe manufacturing and coating at that time with seven plants, but later, it became insolvent. I traveled to Mumbai to meet their director. He said we are OK with Amchem supplying the product, get the vendor's approval, and will proceed. Poker-faced, he also said he would be happy to get our product approved by the brand in other government departments. We were excited about the possibility of a future partnership.

Similarly, Kirloskar Brothers was the EPC for the large-diameter cooling water pipes, about $40,000 m^2$, and BHEL Chennai for the piping close to the boilers. We had made proposals to both and were only awaiting formal NTPC approval. Kirloskar was selling a competing product called Corrocote Glass Flake, and their management was a bit upset at their salespeople for having missed the opportunity.

Our approval was held up for months for unknown reasons. It was as if we had run into a dead wall. Next, we learned that PSL had secured the make water, cooling water, and BHEL packages using an imported polyurethane coating from Copon UK. We were stunned. About a week after that, our approval was miraculously granted, but obviously, it was too late. We had been banking heavily for the past couple of years on these projects fructifying. Welcome to the real world...

The only thing left was the cooling towers, which were about 60,000 square meters per tower, with two towers totaling 120,000 square meters. The pipe coaters were obviously not keen on this work. The package was awarded to the National Building Construction Corp NBCC by NTPC, and the sub-vendor bidding for the Polyurethane Coating work began. During the initial meetings with NBCC, I could gauge that they had an existing favorite vendor supplying them with other products. Although they did not make polyurethane coatings, they came forward to provide it. They made a product data sheet matching the tender specification with test reports. Once bitten and twice shy, I played it differently this time. I put on my best poker face and pretended we were not too keen on the work. In initial pre-tender budgetary estimates, I deliberately gave a high price of $22 per square meter, knowing the price could be leaked. During pre-bid meetings, I would pretend to be totally disinterested in the job and even managed a couple of Oscar-worthy yawns.

The day of the commercial bid opening arrived. I had put extra heavy black paper around the sealed commercial bid in the envelope to prevent access by bright light. I also put my signatures on the sealing surfaces. Then, I covered them with transparent tape so any tampering would be detected. I asked them to check my envelope before they started opening the bids. There was a bit of derisive laughter, and they opened the bids individually.

The Copon-based bid was very high, around $30. An arranged bid to have the mandatory three bids. Or they were out-pricing themselves. The favorite's bid was next to be opened, which was $20, just under our budgetary estimates. There were broad smiles all around the table. It was a done deal. For formality and legal necessity, they opened Amchem's bid. $18 per square metre. Shock all around the table. Faces fell to the floor, but they had no choice. We had won the bid. Went outside and called Raj and Dimple to tell them what had happened. We all had a great laugh. We were finally learning the ropes.

They were not done, though. After some time, NBCC called us and said they had decided to build the two towers together, so they wanted to split the coating order into two with simultaneous work. What a lame excuse. We had seen the site, and the construction work was at least six months apart. Coating something that did not exist. Hmm.. Either we should agree to let go of half, or they would cancel and re-tender in two parts. I guessed the latter option would not have ended well for us, so I reluctantly agreed. Finally, we had only 60,000 square meters out of the total 400,000 square meters in the project, but it was a start.

After all the shenanigans were over, we started getting ready to do the work. A natural draught cooling tower is a vast structure, about 150 meters high or as high as a 50-story building. It is elevated on columns about 10 meters above the ground. It has about 4000 columns and beams supporting the fills, dripping water onto the incoming air. We were supposed to coat everything till about 14 meters high. Such a structure had never been coated in the world, so there was no precedent for logistics and methodology.

Unwrapped Wishes

The plan was to coat the columns and beams outside on ground level with edges exposed. This was a simple task on paper. Then, these members would be erected by NBCC using the central tower crane, and the joints would be manually coated. Raj, Dimple, and a 5-man army shifted to the site near Vishakhapatnam. We planned to hire unskilled people from the side. Coating concrete is hugely complex, as we would learn firsthand soon enough. Unfortunately, there was an accident, and a part of the scaffolding collapsed, leading to some deaths and a significant delay. On resumption, NBCC erected the columns and beams to catch up with the schedule. We would now need to blast clean, prime, and coat the fully erected structure at up to 50 feet height. This changed things from the original plan, and the relatively straightforward task suddenly became complicated.

The site was a mess. Crews erected the beams and fill support. Jointing crews dropped concrete paste and water while we were supposed to work 5 floors directly below. A pebble falling from the top of the tower would have the velocity of a bullet and go through the hard hats and go into your skull. The concrete was full of surface voids, porosity, and honeycombing. Blast cleaning the surface to remove the laitance produced hundreds of bug holes (air voids

on the surface), each of which would make a pinhole defect when sprayed. We solved this by developing a primer on war footing that would foam up in the bug holes by reacting with the moisture in the concrete and filling them up.

NTPC had mandated in our approval that someone from the US counterpart be present on site while we did the coating work. We spoke to them, and Paul Adams came to the site. Paul was a huge, jovial guy. When he arrived at the site, he was warmly welcomed by NBCC and NTPC site staff. He went to the site, looked at the concrete, and declared, "This concrete is not fit for coating." He became persona non grata overnight, and we were told to send him back. However, he did stay for the period we had paid them and was a welcome relief in the situation.

The 60,000 square meters had to be finished in 6 months, or about 400 square meters per day. The main issue was that we had no clue how to coat the elevated areas up to 50 feet above the ground. Scaffolding was not an option. Due to the high-volume output of the machine, spraying each reachable section of the narrow columns would be over in minutes, and the person would need to stop, unhook, and climb to another level. This was just not feasible, as it would be too slow.

Tensions were running high. We were not getting any support from the NBCC site staff in providing proper clean fronts, and the NTPC site staff was often downright rude and offensive. We were not the favorites; they expected someone else to be at the site. Dad flew down to the site to lend support. Like a general in war, he would sit on the site and help with the planning and build morale. During this initial period, while Raj remained unfazed, Dimple became increasingly concerned about the viability of the job. He called me one day, standing in front of the mountain of the tower, and said it just couldn't be done. I don't know where I got it, but I asked him if we could do 400 square meters daily at ground level. Sure, he said. I told him not to look at the whole tower and to focus on the next day's work. We'll find a way to access the upper portions. That calmed him down. Which brings us to the whole point of this chapter. In life, you are faced with enormous tasks and situations, just like a mountaineer standing at the base of Mount Everest. Looking at the peak while climbing will overwhelm you, and you will start thinking it's an impossible task. Look at how much you need to climb that day and achieve that. In time, you will reach the summit.

We ramped up the operations quickly by hiring local staff, many of whom continue to work with us today. Additional equipment was purchased and sent to the site, and more workers were rushed to the site. The Nepali workers were totally unfazed by working at great heights and would simply walk on the narrow beams high up in the air. We had to strictly enforce safety harnessing, which they simply hated.

While Raj and Dimple were tackling the grand challenges at the site, it was my job to ensure coating materials and support from the plant. I was running around crazily between purchase, manufacture, supply logistics, equipment breakdowns, and the whole shebang. Saw many sunrises from my office chair.

During a more extended break, I even added equipment to the plant, which reduced the entire batch cycle to a reasonable 8 hours. We hired a young guy, Shaji Mathew, to look after accounts since Raj was away. He took over some of my load of accounts and banking. The payments were very slow, and I had to juggle postdated cheques to keep funds in check. I asked Shaji to buy me a new pen to sign the cheques. In about two weeks, I started getting calls from the vendors saying that I had issued unsigned cheques! Apparently, it was a disappearing ink pen, and we laughed over it. It could have turned serious, though.

We had to arrange high-reach equipment on an urgent basis. There was no place within the tower to place conventional cranes, and we toyed with several designs of mobile scaffolding. I spoke to several companies to build this, but they were not confident. Just then, I stumbled upon the website of JLG, USA, which sold mobile scissor lifts and articulating booms. A quick check, with bated breath, showed they would fit perfectly within the narrow spaces of the columns. They could elevate quickly, move on to the next grid, and even do up-and-over operations. Seemed like a perfect solution! I called them to see if they had any dealers or equipment available in India. Yes! Escorts was running an access equipment rental division and had some units. I immediately went to meet them. Rentals for the scissors were $3,000 per month; for the boom, $6,000 per month, which was steep back then. They wanted to get out of this business as the demand was low. I negotiated a tremendous hire-purchase deal in which we bought one of each and paid them over eight months. It was almost as much as the rental, and we now owned these.

I immediately signed the contract and asked Escorts to send the equipment to the site. The equipment worked like a charm, and the black clouds lifted. Some workers who did not even know how to drive a car became amazing experts at manoeuvring these inside the very narrow grids. Shortly, we were doing 800 square metres or more a day, but they just could not provide the fronts, except on paper. There were many months of delay. We incurred great costs but were not compensated.

The second tower was almost ready, and we could have finished it in three months flat from the start. Even after watching from the sidelines how we were doing our work, our competitor struggled. They had bought the product from a manufacturer in Himachal Pradesh, and it was experimental. We could

see them put drums on a little fire and start putting this and that chemical inside to change it and try to make it work.

In our scope, we had done a small portion of large-diameter seawater pipelining, about 200 meters in length, from the primary cooling water line to the cooling tower. We blast-cleaned using copper slag, although much cheaper sand was permitted in the specification. Blast cleaning, priming, and coating were done using the automated equipment we developed earlier. The job was flawless, and more than 20 years later, even an inch has not been repaired. Our competitor used sandblasting and manual operations and applied the Copon product without a primer.

The day the plant was started, massive portions of coating from the main CW pipe and some from the MW pipe peeled off and stuck in the condensers, leading to the shutdown. This was removed and thrown away in trucks overnight, but the shutdown continued for several weeks. The Copon product was an elastomeric polyurethane just like ours and needed a primer to bond. I had known this since the day we lost the job and had tried to tell concerned people who would not listen. In those days, every day of the shutdown of a 1000 MW power plant cost $1.5 Million to the utility.

Some years later, LANCO tendered to do a similar project. Of course, we were the first choice to provide technical details on how the work would be done. The commercial bidding day arrived, and we were obviously not the lowest bidder. For the next two days, they called all three bidders together. We would wait outside the conference room, giving each other murderous looks, while they called us in repeatedly one by one. Each was convinced their price had been beaten and they should reduce it further. On the afternoon of the second day, the CEO, did the final negotiations. I was sick of the charade and told him this was my lowest price (about $3 Million), and they could take it or leave it. I explained to him at great length the cost of going for a low-quality vendor, as proved by the Simadhri experience. The lowest bid was about $250,000 less than ours. He said we want to get the job done by you, but you must match the lowest. I refused and walked away. For reasons best known to him, he opted for the inexperienced, low-priced vendor who did a miserable job. I understand the plant had to be shut down for four months due to peeling coating. Back envelope calculations showed a loss of about $20 Million. Excellent decision-making and vision. No wonder they became insolvent in later years.

For Simadhri II expansion, we would work for Kirloskar to line the main CW pipe. Despite being a competitor, they were pleased with our performance and gave us ab excellent customer feedback with glowing reviews. It was big of them.

Due to the significantly increased expense caused by the shift in the coating plan by NBCC, we did not make any money on the project. Instead of compensating us, they did their best to eat up the dues on trumped-up charges. We had a big problem getting our dues out but finally managed after about two years. It would take several chapters if I wrote about it. They were two tough years. At that point, Naren Manocha, Neelu's uncle, invested some money in the company. He stayed with us till 2008 when he decided to sell out and exit. Naren and his wife, Shaila, remain my favorite relatives and are such fun to be with.

It had become a fashion to cut vendors' money on fictional grounds and make extra profits. In the later years, we went on to do many power projects and had to take Reliance Infra and Gammon India to court to get our dues out.

Site contracting work was increasingly becoming unviable since the main contractors had no control over the schedule and would not compensate you for the extra time and cost incurred. In one project for IVRCL, instead of the 5 months contracted, they finished in 32 months and never compensated us. We started using fixed monthly charges (use or pay provisions) in our contracts, which were never appreciated. Most would go for needy vendors who would make up the extra cost by cutting down on quality and material consumption.

Unfortunately, like a Bollywood movie, Polyurethane Coatings became typecast for seawater cooling plants. These were few and far between, and the next project would come up after a decade. There were so many areas in inland power plants where they could be used, but the customer equated them as very high-performance products useful only for highly corrosive seawater-cooled power stations.

IX
LIFE IS BEAUTIFUL

For the next five years, we mostly did LPG Mounded Bullets on a supply-and-apply basis. These were large LPG storage tanks at bottling plants owned by IOCL, BPCL, HPCL, and some others. These were just bread-and-butter businesses that kept the company running. GR Engineering for IOCL at Chengelpet was the first project to be executed. It was a race against time as the monsoons were setting in. Raj and Dimple did a great job finishing the project on time.

Unwrapped Wishes

These projects were "hand to mouth," as one handicrafts exporter jokingly described his business to me many years ago. You would earn some money on a project and survive on that for some time until you ran out of money, and then you needed fresh business. There was no continuous flow of projects in the pipelines.

Neelu, the boys, and I had a great time through all of this. We were always going out to the movies, eating out, pursuing hobbies, simply being happy and enjoying life. We would take a break regularly and head out for a vacation. Sit in the car and drive down the hills of Nainital, Palampur, Shimla, and the like. Or take trips to Goa. Fishing was one hobby of mine that Neelu did not like, but she would still patiently sit by my side reading a book. As the boys grew older, these trips became more frequent, including far-off places worldwide.

Work-life balance has become a subject of much concern nowadays. My take was simple: never take your work home and vice versa. When I reached home, I forgot about work and life would begin. I hated to receive any work-related call at home, and I still do. It is not only the amount of time you spend at work or home; it is the quality.

Travel was always a big passion for Neelu and me. I would surf the internet to search for interesting places to visit. On one such search in 2004, I came across a website of the Meeru Islands in the Maldives. Wow, the place looked out of the world and was simply unreal. I had to go. It was expensive, though, so I had to devise a game plan to make it happen. While the Cochin – Male flights were reasonable, the Delhi – Cochin leg was expensive. We decided to take the 3-day train journey to Cochin and then fly from there. Despite this, the whole trip would cost us $2,200, but the photos were irresistible.

We sat on the train and took off on the long journey. Sometime back, we had bid for an LPG mounded bullet project and were expecting the order on the day we started the journey. We needed to get that job since overdue bank loan installments were to be paid, and we had almost reached the default limit. To my dismay, as we were one hour into the journey, I got a call from the office and was informed that the project had been given to a cheap bidder. I was stunned and brooded for a while on how we would get out of this one.

Then my stoicism philosophy kicked in: Que Sera Sera, whatever will be will be; the future is not ours to see. Life is what eventually happens, not what you imagine will. The following 12 days were some of the most wonderful days of our lives. I never gave work a single thought. We swam in the crystal-clear ocean, snorkeling with amazing marine life, big game fishing, water sports, and eating till we almost passed out. Maldives is what nature was intended to be, totally unspoiled by man. It's terrific and must-do in life.

I took Sachit on a fishing trip early one morning; Aryan was too young to join. Musa and his friend took us on a speedboat in crisp white shirts and blue trousers. It perfectly matched the brilliant white boat and the deep blue sea. We went to a nearby reef and started fishing; the moment the first case hit the water, a bluefin jack took the bait and fought tremendously before we reeled it in. We caught a small Tuna, which Musa decided to use as bait for Barracuda; as we slowly trawled, a shark appeared suddenly and sliced the tuna cleanly into two. Awesome. After two hours, we stopped for Coffee. Musa took out an ice bucket with cakes and pastries, a coffee thermos, White China cups, and saucers, put on white gloves, and served us in the middle of the ocean. This was the life I always wanted.

Life is beautiful. Please don't waste it by being obsessed with work 24 x 7. As many wealthy and successful people have said before their death, they only regretted being obsessed with work, not seeing their children growing up, spending time with family, traveling, hobbies, and passions. I was always clear that was not the route I wanted to take. I could have achieved far more had I just been obsessed with money but was not ready to stop living. Extra achievement is a sacrifice I can make over and over.

X
SINGAPORE CALLING

In the Autumn of 2008, we got a call from Kwong Lee Engineering in Singapore. John Chan, the owner, had seen our website and wanted to use our product for a local project.

The Singapore Public Utilities Board (PUB) was building a unique project called NEWater. This was essentially wastewater that would be treated using special reverse osmosis techniques into ultrapure drinking and industrial water. Singapore faced many water shortages, as it used to import from Malaysia, and the future supply was uncertain. The only way out was to recycle and reuse.

Engineering for the project had been done by a prominent American multinational, CH2M Hill, together with their Singaporean partner, CPG. There was a pipe main line of 2.2 m diameter pipe about 50 miles long for which CH2M had specified polyurethane lining as per American Water Works Association (AWWA) specification C222. Traditionally, PUB used cement mortar lining for such projects, but polyurethane was a faster and better option. At that time, it was the world's largest Polyurethane coating project, so competition was fierce, especially from the American producers.

Unwrapped Wishes

John and I exchanged technical data and pricing. We got our product tested as per stringent Singapore standards for drinking water, SS 375, and it passed with flying colors. He was keen to work with us and proposed our name to PUB and the consultants. There was a lot of opposition. On short notice, we were invited to Singapore to present to PUB, CH2M, and CPG. Dimple, I took the late-night flight to Singapore. We arrived early in the morning and were amazed by the city's beauty and cleanliness. We went to the hotel, showered, and were picked up by John's wife, Rosalind, and son Jonathan. Then, we were taken to the PUB office, a swanky glass tower in the middle of the city. We were pretty groggy since we had not slept the whole night. Although I had given a lot of presentations by then back home, this was the first international one.

Initially, they were hesitant, considering we were a relatively recent entrant and tiny compared to the big American companies vying for the project. I spoke from my heart and satisfactorily answered every conceivable technical question they had. Finally, the team said, "We accept your credentials; you're on." Wow, were we happy, having won this significant contract against stiff international competition?

We then went to the Kwong Lee Factory for a meeting with John Chan and met their daughter, Rachelle. The family was very industrious. The factory was not on the scale we saw in India, and we wondered how John would manage such a massive project in that short a time. When we arrived, Rosalind was operating a forklift, clearing the store for an upcoming visit by PUB. Labour was in short supply in Singapore, and there were many regulations regarding how many overseas workers you could hire. She was a sweet person and, many a time, came to intervene during periods when John became cranky.

Shomendra Mann

In the evening, we had a fabulous dinner in a Michelin-starred restaurant on the top floor of a building overlooking the Singapore skyline. While everyone ordered fancy $100 dishes, I ordered a pizza. Funnily, they all came to take slices from my pizza and weren't too excited about their food. Dimple and I spent the next few days roaming the beautiful city before returning home.

Unwrapped Wishes

After a few days, John and Rosalind came to meet us in India to check out our facility. Our 1000-liter reactor did not inspire much confidence. We had coincidently ordered a 4000-litre bare reactor, which arrived and was kept in the driveway. It had not yet been set up since all the other equipment had not been ordered. I convinced them we would deliver on time, and they agreed to proceed. We went out for dinner at the Radisson, where we signed the contract. The project required us to supply about 680,000 liters of coating.

On the way back home, the enormity of the task struck me. Using the current reactor, we would need to manufacture two shifts per day (16 hours at least), 7 days a week for 38 weeks. There was no time to set up the larger reactor since getting the other equipment and setting it up would take months. The materials purchase and logistics requirements would also be huge. Raj and Dimple would be away in Singapore with our crew, helping Kwong Lee do the spray, so it was up to me only! I felt a cold dread creeping on me. I regained composure and pushed it away. Que sera sera.

The next few months were the hardest we ever worked in our lives, with me in India and them in Singapore. For 22 weeks or about five and a half months, I worked more than 16 hours per day, seven days a week. I would be in the factory at 7:30 AM after dropping the kids off at school, operating the plant, arranging the incoming raw materials, and shipping the goods with a skeleton crew. I would return home by midnight, quickly sleep, and wake up by 6:00 AM. Neelu would visit me in the evening by about 8:00 PM with my packed dinner, stay for a while, and return to the kids. After 22 weeks, things became more manageable as Raj returned and took over the 7:30 PM shift.

In those months, except for the plant and home, I never went anywhere and met no one. It had become so exhausting. Even though I was in my early forties and had tons of energy, there were times when I would lie down on the office floor and tell one of the workers to revive me if I passed out. I longed to take

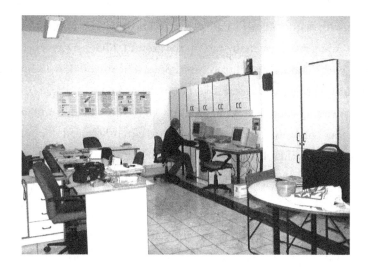

just one day off, sleep, watch a movie, or eat out. You really value life's simple pleasures when you don't have them.

The plus side was we were finally making serious money! Kwong Lee was a great paymaster. During the initial negotiations, John had asked me what it would take to ensure a flawless delivery. Money, I replied, pay us advances in lots. They would happily advance $200,000 or more, which was a great help. Rosalind and I would plan the dispatches and schedule like a war game. Shipments from Indian ports would arrive in about 6 days, which was a great help.

Buying large volumes of materials allowed us to hone our skills in purchasing and imports. Purchasing is the underrated sibling of selling, but it is equally important and often ignored. It can make or break the profitability or competitiveness of your products. Never have a single vendor for any supply. That will slowly erode your profitability. Nothing drives pricing down like healthy competition. Multiple vendors also allow access to newer products and technologies.

Meeting with vendors is also a great way to know what is happening in the industry. You get to have many ears on the ground. I have always encouraged meeting with vendors, even impromptu ones. The interaction always leaves you with something new, even if you don't buy. The right way is to have a friendly meeting where people are encouraged to speak openly and with candor. I cannot count the times people have inadvertently spilled things in meetings that were invaluable for us. Need to know is a fundamental concept in business and, indeed, in life. Sometimes, we need to keep quiet.

John was a tireless worker and unfazed by the challenges he faced. Using simple modifications to his plant, he enhanced its capacity considerably. He was a curious mix of generosity and stinginess, though. One moment, he would drop $20,000 on a new air compressor instead of fixing it; another moment, he would struggle to save the most minuscule of amounts. Once, they suddenly started facing many issues of bubbling in the coating. John started getting angry and blamed the material. Raj and Dimple were foxed; how could one drum from a single batch have quality problems and not the others? Raj discovered that John had ordered flipping the used drums, keeping them open for long periods to drain out every drop of remaining coating. He was collecting these into a single drum and trying to spray that. The coating was absorbing moisture from the air, and it was no surprise that this was foaming up.

Dimple and Raj set up the entire spray line for Kwong Lee. After some initial hiccups, the spray went off smoothly. We had deputed two technicians for the spray, and Kwong Lee had three workers for coating. This small crew took out the entire production. In India, we would have hired three times as many people.

After the coating work was running smoothly in Singapore, Raj and Dimple went to Boon & Cheah, Malaysia, where some of the pipes were being coated, and then on to Bakrie Brothers, Indonesia, where the specials like bends, T's, etc were being fabricated and coated. These were shipped to Singapore on

large barges and erected at the site. Site jointing work also started in Singapore, at times 40 feet below the road level. All in all, it was a lot of work.

XI
THE BUCKET AND THE OVEN

Today, we have an excellent laboratory with great equipment. We also have the finest range of products of any 100% Solids Polyurethane Coatings producer worldwide, bar none. With our wealth of experience and expertise, we can develop bespoke products with a typical turnaround time of 8 weeks, something unheard of in the industry. Going beyond formulations, we are working on new polymer molecules that will be game-changers in the coating industry.

It was not always like this! Early on, I realized that the single-product approach would not last long, especially in the international markets. The original product 386/9000 was multipurpose and used for steel and concrete surfaces. Although it worked exceptionally well in most situations, we needed different properties for many applications. The international producers had moved on to newer technologies like direct-to-metal polyurethanes. We needed to catch up and then develop even better products.

I was fascinated with the coating technology. It became my passion in life. Given my educational background, it was easy to grasp the subject matter. I collected a vast amount of technical data and poured over them. Over the months and years, I began to get a unique perspective of the different chemistries we could use in formulation. I cannot over-emphasize the importance of selecting a particular field in life and focusing on the same. Learn all you can on the subject and build domain knowledge. It is a lifelong exercise that never stops as long as you work. Being passionate about a subject feels like a pet hobby and not work. Today, we have over a thousand technical books on polymers, coatings, and raw materials; to be frank, reading them all is not humanly possible. Fortunately, AI has come to the rescue.

The possibilities to improve were endless. We used six ingredients to cook our dish, but a hundred options were now available. The next step was to acquire samples of the materials for trials. I collected hundreds of them from around the world, cupboards full. The only issue was that we did not have any R&D equipment. We had the requisite batch quality control test instruments prescribed by Exportech but nothing for research and development. There was no budget, so I had to improvise, some of which were hilarious but effective and accurate.

We did not have a tensile tester, so I thought of an alternative. I made end grips from a local machine shop; one end was tied to the reactor crane, the other on a steel bucket with the coating tied in between. Then, I added steel grit slowly to the hanging bucket to add load till the breaking point. Elongation was tested using gauge marks and a handheld shifting steel scale. I would keep one edge on one gauge mark and a close watch on the other. ASTM standard authors would have fainted if they saw the rig, but it was accurate. Much more than the report from the local laboratories.

Hundreds of such tests with my hand gave me great insight into testing. I thoroughly read all the relevant ASTM standards and knew every dot and comma. Other than the equipment, I was strictly following the standards. I had become disillusioned with local laboratories and was pretty sure they had never read the standards or were not following them. In later years, we started relying only on our internal tests and dismissed any lab other than the best international ones.

Lots of the tools I used were kitchen equipment, like mixers. The kitchen mixer did the same job as the fancy laboratory one but cost 1/10th the amount. The equipment that took the cake, however, was my laboratory reactor. A laboratory-scale reaction vessel cost about $10,000 then, so obviously, it was out of the question. So, I purloined the kitchen oven, cut a hole on top, and fitted a motor with the mixer blade. Put a thermocouple to measure the reaction temperature and a nitrogen inlet fed by a cylinder. It was just as good! I must have done a few hundred reactions in this jig. I was ably supported by my laboratory assistant, Lal Babu. He used to drive a rickshaw until I hired him as a laborer at our plant. Of course, his job was to clean the equipment and pass me things, so his educational background did not matter. The funniest thing about Lal is that he is a repeater. I would say, 'Let's heat it more,' and he would say, 'Let's heat it more'. It was hilarious, and I often say nonsensical things for comic relief. He still works in our factory but not in the lab.

The bad part about the lab was that it was situated in an open area just next to the reactor. There were only two counters, and it was open within the shed. It was miserably hot in summer, and after about an hour, I used to get covered in sweat from head to toe. I had to return to my office to dry out and cool down. The color of my face would go back from red to a more normal shade. I would shift the instrument to my office for tests requiring room temperature. As you can imagine, winters were a much better season for my research than summers. No wonder the first equipment I bought when we got some extra funds was an air conditioner for the laboratory! In hindsight, though, the cooling-off period was a blessing in disguise as I would return to my computer and attend to important things like buying and selling. If not, I would have spent most of my time in the laboratory.

Every reaction was documented, all data was meticulously filed on the computer, and I made Excel charts with trend lines. Over time, patterns started emerging, and I understood how each raw material would affect the polymer, both positively and negatively.

After a decade of doing this, I could look at the requirements, make the formulation in my head, put the calculations on paper, and most often, it worked just as expected. Over the years, we have made use of this knowledge. We designed the highest performing coatings for different sectors direct to metal pipeline coatings, coatings for ductile iron, concrete lining, aliphatic solvent-free polyurethanes, and such, all exceeding international standards such as American Water Works Association AWWA, European EN, International ISO, British BS, French, Singapore, etc. My principal aim was always to make the highest-performing coating, exceeding anything in the market. Low-cost, mass-market products never interested me.

Sachit, my elder son, has a keen interest in the subject, and so does my laboratory staff. Sachit played a significant role in developing the Drythane and Amshield range. Whatever I learned during the years is being passed on to them. All research work is under my control, as I love to do this work even today.

In today's world, technology is the biggest differentiator, not capital. I see large companies struggling to innovate and produce newer-generation products. The research and development should report directly to the owners so that the path forward is focused and decision-making is quick. Large corporations work like a bureaucracy with an extremely slow decision-making process. Our turnaround time for new product development is typically 10 weeks compared to around 18 months for larger companies in our field; no wonder they are forever trying to acquire smaller specialist companies with the promise of letting the founders continue to run the place. We have received many offers from major international companies over the years but have never been interested.

Raj and Dimple were busy with their passions, Dimple with equipment and construction, and Raj with finance and administration. Both burned the midnight oil in learning various aspects and intricacies. Our skills in all aspects of the business grew steadily, and a sustainable business emerged. We did not have middle management, and I used to joke that our Army was weird: one chief, three generals, and only soldiers—no ranks in between. The generals did all the work of the brigadiers, colonels, majors, lieutenants, and NCOs. The workload was huge, but we managed. The major plus of this arrangement was that decisions were made with lightning speed. Clients would be awe-struck when our answers and bids would arrive within the hour instead of days, which they were used to. We realized that we three had different skills that were not available with the other, so we ultimately left specific work to the person with the most skill in that area. This system continues to date with complete confidence that the work will be done.

For the next decade, we made inroads into new sectors and established leadership in each field: pipeline rehabilitation, mounded bullets, cooling towers, seawater pipelines, sewage treatment plants, etc. Each area had its share of unique challenges and requirements, but our combined skills and total dedication helped us overcome them and succeed.

Amchem has undoubtedly created the 100% Solids Polyurethane Coatings market in India and in many ways worldwide.

XII
To Save a Penny

The most obvious way to end up with money is to earn it, but we sometimes overlook the second way: save and invest. Almost all the money we earned went back into the business, and we lived a relatively simple life. People must have speculated, but I never cared about displaying. We would get much more happiness from buying a great piece of machinery or Land, practically nothing from an expensive watch or the like. These things were alien to our culture. Being raised in an Army household, money was never a significant factor in our lives. Sure, we had big houses, help, good food, and a great social life, but there was no excess money. Saving and reinvesting in the business enabled the creation of significant assets, such as capacity and capability, over the years.

Most people who end up rich never really blow up their money. Some people earned a lot and did not know how to save, so they ended up badly. There are many horror stories of movie stars, sportspeople, and the like who earned millions yet ended up practically on the street by spending obscene amounts on ridiculous things.

I'm not propagating miserliness; that extreme is equally bad, if not worse. One of the primary purposes of earning money is to have a comfortable living and do things like travel, a lovely house and car, good food, and generally having a good life without the stress of how to pay for basic things like health. If you don't do that, money is nothing but big numbers in your bank account. There is no point in justifying miserliness by 'leaving for the next generation.' If you pay for the future generations, what should they do with their lives? Drugs, alcohol, and parties? Is that what you want for your children and grandchildren?

Financially, too, it is wise to buy assets and use them rather than rent. This is not applicable in all economies but certainly in growing ones. The asset is quietly earning for you in the background, without procurement or production issues, quality, staff, or unpaid dues issues. After many years, you are pleasantly surprised at how much the asset has silently earned when you finally sell it to move on or expand. We sold our first factory land for 100X of cost! The rising value of assets is also a great way to build collateral for funding bank loans. It is an excellent arbitrage tool, borrow cheaply, gets higher returns via capital appreciation through the assets, and even pays lower taxes. That's how the rich get hugely wealthy, not from revenue but from assets. Curiously, even lending banks do not appreciate these aspects and are primarily focused on earning projections and ratios.

In this chapter, I will share some techniques we can use to invest and create wealth. Most people look at investing as a very complex idea beyond their capability. It's not that complicated, and I will focus only on simple but fundamental concepts. Astute investors will already know what I will write about. You don't need to be a Wall Street investment banker to make money. That stuff has gone crazy and entirely out of hand. I have some unconventional ideas on wealth, primarily generational passed-on land assets, which die-hard capitalists would consider radical.

Savings are the first part. The adage of 'save 30% of what you earn' seems reasonable. Ideally, you should be able to survive on 70% of what you earn. You may need to give up a few frills in the initial years till some excess builds up. Even if you start small, start. Acorns grow into big oak trees in time. If you never plant the seed, nothing will grow. Don't wait till you have what you consider an investible surplus.

The next step is to get a return for the money, an increment year after year. A slight 5% or even 10% return doesn't sound much. Let's invest $1,000 only once. Even a 10% return is only $100 in a year, which is nothing to get excited about. *The magic is in compounding;* the following year, you get a return on the principal plus interest and so on in the coming years. Over the years, it becomes serious money. The longer you stay and the better rate you can manage, the exponentially bigger the end-of-term amount gets. Let's look at a few scenarios.

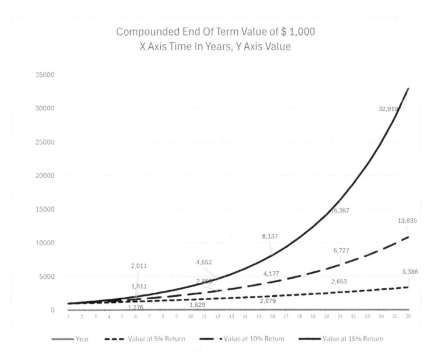

Unwrapped Wishes

It's incredible how much the initial amount of $1,000 becomes. You can see how the term and the rate of return make such a huge difference! If you start investing only $1000 *per year* over the next 30 years, it becomes the following:

Return	Total Invested	End Of Period Value
At 5%	$ 30,000	$ 74,082
At 10%	$ 30,000	$ 198,392
At 15%	$ 30,000	$ 566,168

Now let's say you invest $5,000 per year, it becomes

Return	Total Invested	End Of Period Value
At 5%	$ 150,000	$ 370,413
At 10%	$ 150,000	$ 991,964
At 15%	$ 150,000	$ 2,830,843

So, if you start investing only $5,000 a year at the age of 25 and manage a 10% annual return, by the time you retire at 55, you will have a million dollars in savings! Didn't I say it was magic?

But. There is always a but! Inflation eats away at the value of your money, and the actual value of your money at the end of the period is lower. The number of the same things you can buy with the cash is lesser. But if you invest wisely, you can get around this. You just need to focus on the net, inflation-adjusted return rate. Return and inflation will depend on the type of economy of your country. The return is low in developed economies, but so is inflation, and vice versa for developing countries!

Quick aside to developed countries, invest in countries with growth, don't struggle with 2-3%. For example, let's take where I stay, India, a developing country. Typical values would be:

Type of Return	Basic Return	Inflation Rate	Nett. Return
Bank Deposit	7%	5%	2%
Stock Indices	12%	5%	7%
Undeveloped Land	16%	5%	11%

Again, going back to invest $1,000 only once, the real value becomes

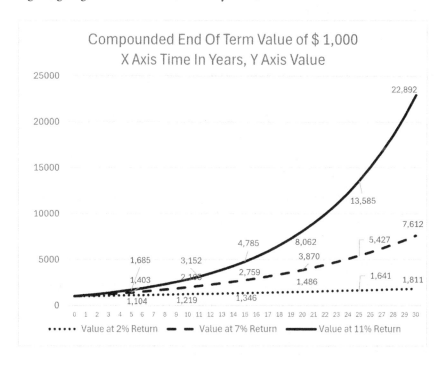

Now let's say you invest $5,000 per year, it becomes

Nett Return	Total Invested	End Of Period Value, Inflation Adjusted
At 2%	$ 150,000	$ 215,954
At 7%	$ 150,000	$ 543,426
At 11%	$ 150,000	$ 1,219,027

That's why I simply detest bank deposits and bonds. You are only allowing your hard-earned money to be used by banks and borrowing corporations to make money while you end up with peanuts. The nett rates of return are historical values, so it's not fiction. In fact, you could end up with better returns if you choose wisely. I'm not taking risky bets, just wiser bets. Let's look.

The valuation of every asset is a game of demand and supply: stocks, Land, gold, and everything in between. Pick up the supply when the demand is low and exit when the demand is high. I'm not talking about timing the markets, though. That stuff is risky and playable only when you have deep pockets, understanding, and a risk appetite. We just need to understand the fundamentals and move accordingly. The average person has several investment opportunities: stocks, gold, real estate, and such. We must continuously diversify. It's tempting to stay only in one area, especially if it has recently given you a good return. However, some avenues intermittently remain static for periods that can last even a decade. Holding a diversified portfolio will help you overcome this challenge. Also, many of these have interrelated returns; for example, if stocks fall due to fear, gold invariably rises as people put money into a safer heaven.

Stocks: What is stock? You simply become the owner of a small piece of a company. The company borrows money from a bank (your bank deposit), adds manufacturing or service value, and ends with a higher profit than the cost of the debt. Returns are, therefore, inherently much higher than debt. Even if the profits are not distributed through a dividend and reinvested in more assets and production capability, you own a share, the book value of which increases accordingly. There is practically no risk here unless the company makes losses, and you lose proportionately. This can be covered by diversification into many companies and sectors. Some companies or sectors do better than others, intermittently, and you can better return. The question is, do you understand balance sheets and can you keep track of how companies are performing? For most passive investors, this is not possible, so we must rely on index funds or mutual funds, which hold a diverse pool of select stocks. For active investors with a more significant risk appetite, you can have a more proactive approach.

Index Funds or Mutual Funds: The safest way to use the stock market is as an investor, not a speculator. Just invest money you do not need for foreseeable periods in Index or Mutual Funds and hold on to them. NEVER borrow to invest in stocks. Funds are a very safe avenue if you do not make knee-jerk reactions of selling when the markets fall. Just close your eyes, don't watch stock news. Using the compounding effect, you will get an excellent return over a long period of time.

As an example, let's analyze the historical monthly closing data for the Indian Sensex from 1980. In 44.75 years, it went from 123.45 to 84,299.74, a compounded annual growth rate of 15.70%. It looks pretty doable now, doesn't it?

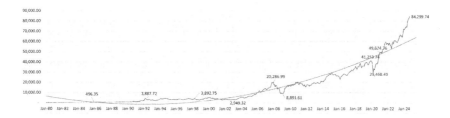

However, if you want to maximize returns and are not very risk-averse, you can keep an overall watch on the markets and enter and exit during extremes of fear or euphoria. I'm not taking daily or even monthly trading. That is a sure-fire way to lose money. I'm talking about making use of extreme cycles, which happen every 5-8 years or so.

Rises and falls are inherent in stocks. The fundamental nature of supply and demand for a particular stock drives its price up or down. However, there are periods when the entire market is much higher or lower than the 'normal', depending on sentiment or external factors such as political uncertainty, looming conflicts, pestilence, etc. We can keep track of this variation and act; the polynomial trendline shows where the 'normal' progression should have been and the overall situation at a particular time.

In recent decades, retail investors, high-net-worth individuals, investment firms, and banking channels have been pumping money into the stock markets instead of bonds and deposits due to low returns. This high demand and low supply have created unrealistic valuations, which are supported by even more speculative inflows. Everyone is happy and these bogus valuations are the new normal despite having no ground reality in earnings.

The markets rise to dizzying levels, and then the large, experienced players cash out. Speculators, especially retail ones, are very emotional, especially when their portfolio loses some value. They panic to avoid further losses and sell, compounding the sentiment. The conventional wisdom is not to time the markets, which is true for most passive investors. They should keep investing in a systematic investment plan SIP and stay for long periods, which overrides the frequent roller coasters. Seeing self-proclaimed individual experts doing day trading or short trades, futures, and options is amusing. A great majority will lose their parent's money. First-time lucky speculators become firmly convinced that they have some special inborn talent, which gives them a unique perspective on stock trade selection. They all soon realize their folly. How can anyone predict the short-term movement of the markets?

What you can track, however, is whether the entire market is fairly valued, undervalued, or overvalued. This is done by tracking historical valuations and gauging how the predictive valuations compare to the current one. If you can keep track of these trends, you can buy extra stocks during periods of irrational fear, sell out parts during times of euphoria, and keep the cash for a saner day to return to the market.

Let's look at some examples of crashes from over the years, starting with 2008.

The Fall of 2008

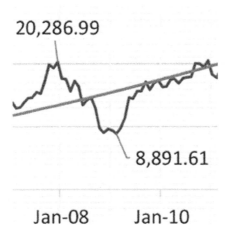

As per the Indian Sensex trendline, stocks were overvalued. Similarly, the US stocks were overvalued. You could have sold since the shift upwards from usual was significant. Even if you did not, you could have bought when there was a substantial fall below expected valuation. Buy additional amounts and return to holding. I did that with money from the Singapore project and made a tidy bundle.

The Fall of 2020

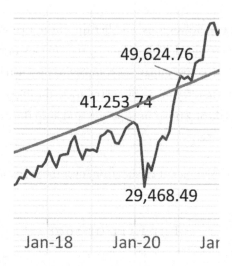

The markets were reasonably priced, but COVID-19 happened, and it crashed. Although the world wasn't going to end, it felt like that. If the world had ended, your stock portfolio would be useless to you anyway, so there was no point in selling. There was so much fear that the market crashed, especially mid-cap and small-cap. The figure alongside is of the Sensex index. I was buying stock left, right, and center from home while doing senseless things like cleaning walls. I can still hear the background music of CNBC playing from bell to bell.

When the world returned to normal within a year, I made 3X of my investments. Of course, they went up to 5X later, but no complaints. You can never time the peak accurately.

The Fall of 2024 & 2025

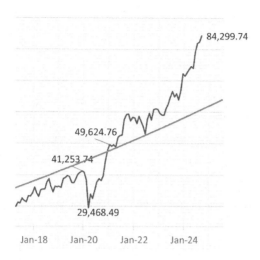

When writing this, October 2024, I can already see a massive crash coming since the market is grossly above my beloved red line. According to the trendline, the Sensex should be around 60,000, but as of September 2024's closing, it was 84,300, or about 40% overvalued. The eagerness of the new retail investor has primarily caused this.

As per Securities Exchange Board of India SEBI data of 170 million DEMAT accounts, 130 million have been opened post-Covid, with 63.6 million in the last two years alone. Retail investors are putting money into the market like there is no tomorrow. Overvaluation is bound to be followed by correction. Unfortunately, when markets tend to correct, the retail investor panics and exits in droves, compounding the issue. If it happens, I hope the sane remains invested for another three years. The markets will come back to their actual value. If you stay, losses are notional; if you sell, the losses are actual. One trick worth doing when you are losing a lot notionally is to dump everything, incur an actual loss for tax, and rebuy everything the same day. The loss can be adjusted against future gains.

I've sold everything for over a year, waiting for the crash or, as some would politely call it, a significant correction. The bulls would call this blasphemous.

Back to Assets

Land: Buying real estate, especially Land, is a perfect choice in a developing economy with a growing population. It would be a significant losing proposition in places like Japan, where the population is shrinking. Land is finite, and unlike money, you cannot print it. The newer generation needs Land for homes, industries, schools, hospitals, etc. My pet peeve is that wealthy speculators have grabbed and are holding on to most of the accessible Land, making it extremely expensive and out of the reach of the next generation. I firmly believe we should have restrictions on freehold land ownership. I will discuss this later, but let me dwell on how the investment works.

Like every investment, it's all about demand and supply. When supply is limited, and the place has high demand, prices shoot up. The key to investment in real estate is to look at areas where there is abundant supply and little demand now, but in the foreseeable future, there will be population growth and higher demand. There is very little point in buying central locations at sky-high prices and expect even higher prices. There is a limit on how much any industry can pay for a factory land yet be profitable. In the same way, there is a limit on how much people can spend from their incomes to have a home of their own.

One of the best ways to look at locations is to see aerial views on Google Maps and Earth to see the direction of the population and ongoing development. You can see hidden gems. We picked up some great places this way. Planned highways and places en route may be excellent choices. In real estate, there is a gestation period where, for many years, prices remain static and then suddenly start shooting up when the place gets populated. In my experience, five to eight years seems to be the usual period. You need to hold for this period, but the returns are well worth the wait, in the 16-22% range.

The only limiting factor is that often, it is a big-ticket investment that could be out of reach until you have accumulated a particular corpus. In the middle of 1990, I had this idea of people getting together and buying real estate on a proportionate share basis, much like a mutual fund. Real estate investment trusts REITs became a reality in India only in 2019. There are now four of these in India; some have yielded a good return of 20-30% in the past few years. This seems to be a good way out going forward.

Gold & Silver: Like Land, gold and silver are limited. This alone makes them inherently valuable. Gold has given 9.28% CAGR over the last 75 years, and silver has given 4.03% over the past 45 years. Returns have been traditionally not very high, but safety and liquidity are excellent. In my opinion, these are set to grow significantly, as seen in the past few years.

In 1971, the USA went off the gold standard, which meant the interconvertibility of currency to gold ended. The American government would guarantee the dollar, so the concept of Fiat currency started when they could simply print money backed by absolutely nothing. Others followed suit. This, combined with the petrodollar, where crude oil was allowed to be traded only in US Dollars, has created the most enormous windfall in history for the US. In recent years, the other emerging large economies of the world have become determined to end the US Dollar hegemony as the world reserve currency and create alternative international currencies backed by, most likely, gold. The BRICS nations are at the forefront of this move and have bought large quantities of gold to build reserves. Eighty-four more countries are ready to sign up. If this happens, gold will skyrocket much more than the increase witnessed in the past few years. I would trust only physical gold, not bank gold bonds. That's another paper IOU.

Unwrapped Wishes

Silver is now in high demand for solar panels, batteries, semiconductors, and other such devices, and its value has grown significantly in recent years. If the demand continues to surge, the pricing will soar. In the past 12 months, this has increased more than 30%.

XIII
Growing The Company

After the Singapore NEWater project, sectors such as pipeline rehabilitation, mounded bullets, cooling towers, seawater pipelines, sewage treatment plants, and so on started producing a regular revenue stream. We had finally become a sustainable business.

However, since we had to apply the product on all the projects, our growth in terms of sales volume remained lower than expected. The challenges of site application, the lack of timely project completion by our customers, and payment issues made us realize that we had to move on to other avenues that were not tied to the application. This was a tough call as these specialized 2K polyurethanes were closely tied to a proper application to be a success. Many coating companies have tried to use the licensed applicator model where third-party coating contractors made the application. In most cases, this turned out to be a disaster.

Two potential areas seemed very promising. One was pipeline coating, where the volume was huge, and the pipe mill had to deliver specific quantities in a time-bound schedule. In addition, their crews were far more skilled and capable than coating applicators. Since they did not have polyurethane coatings experience, we could initially step in with our equipment and crews. The problem was that the pipeline coating industry, especially in India, was not using polyurethane coatings but conventional products such as 3-layer polyethylene, fusion bond epoxies, etc. Polyurethanes were unknown in the Indian market.

The other issue was production speed. The traditional coatings were done in large plants where blast-cleaned pipes were coated continuously, one after the other, on a skew conveyor with a large daily production of more than 5000 square meters per day. On the other hand, polyurethane coatings were applied to a turning pipe roll. After each pipe was coated, it had to be lifted and left to dry and replaced with another pipe. All this took quite a while, and the production was 500 square meters or less daily. It was not economically viable for the pipe mills to use the coating. For the polyurethane to be coated on the skew conveyor, it had to be hard dry in seconds, enough to take the weight of the multi-ton pipe without damaging the coating. Plus, the elastomeric Polyurethane technology required a primer, which would take an hour to cure before the top coat could be applied. The mills just did not have enough time to use a primer. It had to be direct to metal (DTM).

At the risk of sounding immodest, the way we got the market is a business school textbook case. The first step was to develop the product to meet all the requirements. I had been experimenting for years with hundreds of formulations and trials. We were almost there, but some other properties did not meet the design requirements. One issue was that the coating needed to be polar to bond directly to the steel, and polar polymers would absorb water. We fast-tracked the research and finally came up with the perfect chemistry. It met all the requirements: high performance, fast cure, no primer, and very low water absorption and cathodic disbondment.

Although the product tested very well, we had never applied this in real life in a pipe coating plant. As usual, we spoke to the biggest pipe mill, sent sample drums, and landed up for the trials. On the way, I was getting nightmares of the pipe skidding and sliding on the skew conveyor, the coating still not hard dry. As it happened, it went off like a dream. Honestly, I had thought it would take many more trials to get it to work well. All fingers crossed behind my back may have had an effect.

The next step was to identify customers, prepare techno commercial comparative, life cycle cost analysis, and all such data. Then we went on the road. My nephew Rizvaan and I went all over the country over a couple of years, talking to users, consultants, and pipe mills, meeting people, and giving presentations. Some forward-thinking departments adopted the know-how, and we started doing significant projects with this new technology. It quickly beat all other coating systems in the market due to sheer quality, productivity, cost, and environmental reasons such as low energy and water consumption. We had tied up bulk supply contracts for all the raw materials from leading producers in the world and were able to give excellent prices. It took over 90% of the water pipe market in the coming years and is still the market leader. Several cheap imitation products are on the market now, but they just do not perform.

Another application we quickly made using this new technology: the ductile iron (DI) pipe market. We had been talking to DI pipe manufacturers for some time, but even they had all the same checkboxes to tick. The original products we made did not, but the new ones did. As usual, the trials were conducted in the middle of a major producer's factory with dozens of eyes looking at the pipe. I had sweaty palms. The external coating worked precisely as designed, and we were in!

The internal lining was a bigger challenge. When I saw the surface of the freshly cast pipe, it reminded me of the back of a crocodile shot a hundred times by a BB gun. I initially thought that there was no way this surface could be coated without a pinhole. So we began with a series of experiments on how to tackle the issue. The first was to grind away the slag and produce a relatively even surface, followed by blast cleaning. We made a makeshift pipe rotator in the plant, bought several ductile iron pipes from the market, and tried many formulations, pipe rotation speeds, and coating setting speeds. I was getting convinced that it could be done. After many trials, it worked, and we got a glass-like smooth surface without any pinholes. I must have collected a lot of coating on

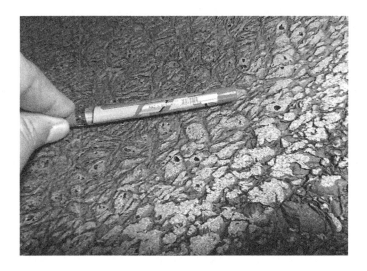

me in the process, but doing things with my own hands is something that I love to do. There has been a lot of skin peeling off my hands over the years.

We had always been thinking of getting into the widespread retail construction market. In 1997, we did a roof waterproofing for an uncle using the original spray applied 386/9000. He had grown a lawn and garden on top and many times causally commented on how well it was working. So, I decided to look at the condition of the coating, which has been in service for more than 20 years. Wow, it was in pristine shape. We then decided to develop a range of high-performing coatings for waterproofing that could be DIY roller-applied and still perform as well as the spray-applied industrial ones. Limiting to spray application would mean limiting the market reach.

Sachit, my elder son, joined the company around the same time in 2017 and was tasked with developing the range. He christened the trade name Drythane, and we started working on the formulations. Like a chip of the old block, he spent many months in the lab and field doing trials based on what I had initially suggested. Many variants later, we launched our first product in the range, Drythane Standard, and he started approaching the customers. It was

Unwrapped Wishes

an instant hit due to its sheer performance and reasonable price. Over the years, we have expanded the range to include high elongation variants, spray Polyurea, and Hybrids, as well as an excellent flooring range we named Amshield Deck. The performance is way better than anything else in the market, and we are poised to launch even better products in the coming months based on entirely new chemistries.

In the last few years, we have also developed many new innovative and novel products in the Purethane range: spray place pipe, high elongation lining for bolted tanks, color-fast coatings, hybrid polyurea for specialized applications such as high abrasion, etc. They are all uniquely high-performing. Amchem now has the broadest range of high-performing polyurethane coatings in the world, with each product being very distinct and designed to serve a particular purpose.

In each case, the same process was followed: identify the customer's needs, understand the quality of products available in the market, develop high-performance formulations, and conduct thorough proving trials before launching commercially. This is standard. The one thing I have realized is that you achieve results only by doing, not by planning. Don't kill ideas by overplanning and overthinking what could go wrong. Trials show you what works, what does not, and what needs improvement or change. Like Nike says, "Just Do It".

During all this growth, we also had to set up the team and systems to run the much larger and expanding business. We had no formal business education, so we were not even very sure how companies were structured, and I had even Googled about it. But using the common-sense approach, we set up the structure, research, purchasing, operations, quality control, marketing, sales, human resources, and administration. Hiring people and setting up systems. The generals finally created a hierarchy, and they were getting on in years. At some stage, every entrepreneur needs to pause doing things himself and learn how to manage people who do as you plan. This was and, in many senses, remains one of the most challenging tasks.

It's never too late to learn, and there will always be people who know much more than you about a particular aspect. Leave your ego at the door and learn from them. A couple of years ago, at 58, I enrolled in online business classes run by a business coach, Rajiv Talreja. Rajiv has met and studied over 300 owners and CEOs of the biggest and most successful companies and teaches you what he learned from them. He is highly passionate and committed to his work, and taking part in his essential and advanced courses gave me further clarity on how to proceed with our systems. His enthusiasm is infectious, and he can speak and teach continuously for 8 hours with the audience struggling and unable to match his energy. Thank you, Rajiv. You are doing an excellent job for society.

A company is only as good as the people who work there. You need to find passionate and committed people with dreams and goals. Well, every potential employee shows this during the interview. I wonder which training school they go to. Once they start, the massive decline begins, and you start wondering what made you hire them or even if you are unskilled at hiring people.

On the other hand, there are not-so-impressive people you hire who turn out to be fabulous workers. Some very young and inexperienced people we hired became the company's bedrock. They had unwavering loyalty and dedication and had been with us for over 25 years. Nilesh in accounts, Ganesh in manufacturing, and Shubrat in administration have been the bedrock. Many potential superstars we hired have either faded away or left for a higher package without much contribution to the company. I've tried many scientific methods, tests, and assessment factors to determine suitability, but they have mostly failed. I guess you can go with a gut feeling, and if things are not working out in the reasonable amount of time it takes to impart skills, you need to let them go. This may seem harsh, but I think getting a divorce is better than staying in a bad marriage for years together. It's painful, but both parties benefit by separating.

The next most important thing is to impart skills. The employee will not have the domain knowledge at the beginning and will take time to learn, settle, and contribute. This is a painful process; you spend hundreds of man-hours of training, and in many cases, they will just not pick up or, worse yet, leave for the next better offer. I have personally spent hundreds of hours imparting skills that were completely wasted in the end. Now, I've just started treating it as a part of corporate life and accepting it as an inevitable evil.

Systems are a very crucial part of a business. They allow running of complex organizations and operations relatively smoothly and minimise errors. However, very complex systems result in an unwieldy bureaucracy detrimental to efficiency. In today's world, businesses must be very quick on their feet to tackle rapid changes in the market and, more importantly, be the ones who create the change. Systems could be considered guidelines, and we must trust and give staff the freedom to make changes, keeping circumstances in mind.

Shomendra Mann

The Future

The future of Amchem is full of potential and, in equal measure, challenges, just like the world. We have matured into a research-oriented, goal-driven, and environmentally responsible company. Technology is at the heart of our operations. We now have scale and are further expanding rapidly. Already about half of our sales are in international markets. We aim to become, in the next few years, internationally the first choice for the products we manufacture and the industries we serve. This is already true in many areas, but we have barely scratched the market's surface. There is a potential problem crying for a solution wherever I look. As we advance, we will continue to address the customers' pain points and use technology in design and production to address them. We hope to hire and onboard enough committed and hard-working people to achieve this goal. In the future, that seems to be the biggest challenge. One thing life has taught me is that there is no alternative to hard work if you want to achieve something big.

We are developing coating technologies that could enable quantum jumps in performance. Going far beyond formulations, we are developing new polymer molecules that will provide solutions hitherto not possible. We plan to roll them out in the next months and years.

AI will be the big disruptor, the effects of which are difficult to predict. It will accelerate human knowledge and capability to extraordinary levels. It is inevitable, and nothing can stop the advance. What is dangerous is the complete control by just a few corporations and zero government oversight. Politicians are simply dumbfounded bystanders looking and wondering what is going on.

Societies that adopt this technology will leapfrog ahead, and those that do not will continue at present growth and development rates. However, adopting societies will also lose employment in fields that rely purely on knowledge and reasoning. This loss will be far more significant when AI merges with robotics since manual labor, mainly factory production workers, will be affected. The corporates and Moghuls who control the technology will reach trillions in personal wealth while the unemployed will struggle to survive.

Universal Basic Income (UBI) will simply not be possible (who will pick up the tab?) or enough of a counter as humans need a sense of purpose to thrive. Loss of real-world jobs will also adversely affect the economy and the demand for goods and services – a double-edged sword. If there are very few car customers (many unemployed people), what will be the point of making automated, robotic factories? This has the potential to unleash civil unrest, and governments across the globe will be forced to enforce regulations to prevent such a significant loss of employment. In my view, these events will be felt far more in developed societies than in developing economies where people are far from adopting these technologies.

In a more optimistic view, AI will seamlessly and slowly integrate with society and work wonders for humans. I wish and secretly believe this will ultimately be the case. Aryan, my younger son and gifted genius is in the thick of the AI world in San Francisco. He's constantly educating me on the latest developments in AI and teaching the old dog new tricks. Fortunately, this old dog loves new tricks, and I'm seamlessly adopting all the new technologies. AI will help us solve one of my biggest concerns for the future. All my research work over the years was stored in my brain cells. How would this get transferred to the next generation? Although I have thousands of technology files on my computer, reading text is insufficient to distil all this into usable knowledge. Data sets created based on our experiments will be converted by AI into logical reasoning and the creation of new products. All this will be ably supported by me till I can, and then Sachit and our research team. We will be doing it in days, which used to take months. And with far better results. The future looks fantastic.

XIV
Annexure

Like everyone, I'm concerned about some of the things going on in the world and the direction they are headed. I want to share my concerns and suggest concrete steps forward. Since these are my personal views and have nothing to do with the Amchem story. Ideally, this should have been in another book. However, I'm not likely to write another one since I'm not an author and will be busy with the next phase of the company's growth and my own life. If you have read this far, you are likely to understand how I view the world. Keeping that in mind, please consider the following pages slowly and deliberately. Try to reflect on the issues I raise and the solutions I offer and see where we agree or disagree. We are all responsible for raising our voices to improve things in society and cannot remain the silent majority forever. Please be vocal about these issues and be a part of forcing the change.

Unwrapped Wishes

The Emperor's New Clothes

As a child, I read a story. An emperor, obsessed with fine clothing, hires two swindlers who claim they can make him a magical suit invisible to those unfit for their roles. The emperor, not wanting to appear unworthy, pretends to see the clothes, as do his officials. He parades through town in his "new clothes" until a child shouts the truth: he's wearing nothing. The emperor realizes he's been deceived but continues his parade, choosing pride over truth.

In a sense, we are in the same situation. Our hubris may end up being our downfall. We have made significant progress over the years and centuries as a civilization. We have food, shelter, medicine, transportation, and leisure that earlier man could have never imagined. But there are so many things going wrong that we must look at and correct. I want to give my simple take on a few things.

Political Systems & Democracy

We have come a long way in how we run our society and have experimented with all kinds of systems: monarchy, theocracy, communism, and democracy. (I believe presidential systems don't fit well in modern times. While having one leader can speed up decision-making, it also means we rely solely on that person's judgment, ability, and mental fitness—which can lead to serious problems). Democracy is the best system so far, but in the past few decades, the chinks have started showing up. I'm not suggesting we find another system; things must be modified.

Democracy is based on the ideal notion of 'of the people, by the people and for the people' as enunciated by Abraham Lincoln. People would elect their representatives, and they, in turn, would run the system solely for the benefit of the people. Somewhere along the line, this has become topsy-turvy. Representatives have become professional politicians who use every trick in the book to win. Hatred, divide, fear-mongering, pandering, religion, monetary sops, reservation, and such have become tactics to win. These negatives still sway most people's minds, so they become misguided by these considerations, forgetting what the elected representatives should deliver. The 24/7 bombardment of agendas by the media and social media has accentuated the problem.

Elections have now become a game of money power, controlled media, and hidden corporate donors, PACs, Super PACs, and lobbyists. After being elected, the representatives serve the interests of corporations and vested interests or spend time creating and perpetuating their fiefdoms and legacy. Ordinary people are suffering with slight tangible improvement in their lives. In most developed countries, the average worker, fireman, teacher, farmer, and the like is much worse off than decades ago. No wonder people are desperately clutching at straws being offered by populist leaders promising them a better future. They have nothing concrete to offer, and things will likely worsen before society is forced to make changes.

We are aghast at hearing about some politicians worldwide, their crudity and apparent lack of civility and character, and the absence of domain knowledge required to take society forward. However, the politicians come from within our society; they are our people, so there is little point in pointing fingers personally and showing disgust and disdain. The capability is questionable even with the slim chance that the politician is working for altruism. They have the power over the educated and capable civil services but without much domain knowledge. This is not to say that the bureaucracy does a fantastic job, just that it can, given the right circumstances and powers.

The conclusion is inescapable since this is a worldwide phenomenon: the system is faulty and needs to change. Recent studies show that voter disenfranchisement and rising income inequality are not isolated issues but symptoms of a deeper, systemic problem. Data from several democracies indicate that as public trust in government erodes, the gap between those in power and ordinary citizens widens. This trend suggests that unless there is a concerted effort to reform campaign finance laws, boost transparency, and encourage genuine civic participation, the cycle of corruption and neglect will only continue to grow.

Let's do a refresher on what an elected government is supposed to deliver to the people in an ideal world:

Law and Order: Maintain justice, enforce laws, and ensure public safety.

National Defence: Protect the country from external threats and maintain armed forces.

Public Infrastructure: Build and maintain roads, bridges, public transportation, and utilities (water, electricity, etc.).

Healthcare: Provide access to healthcare services and ensure public health.

Education: Ensure access to quality education for all citizens.

Social Welfare: Help people who are struggling by offering programs like welfare, unemployment benefits, and social security.

Economic Stability: Encourage a growing economy, control rising prices, and create job opportunities.

Environmental Protection: Put in place rules to protect nature and use our natural resources wisely.

Foreign Relations: Build and maintain good relationships and trade connections with other countries.

Public Services: Ensure everyone has access to basic services like cleaning, waste management, and emergency help.

Politicians should only discuss concrete agendas and plans for these issues. Instead, we are constantly, and intentionally, sidetracked by divisive topics.

The reform discussion needs to be started and pushed by civil society and the media. The physician will not heal himself! Unfortunately, most media is now controlled by corporations with vested interests, so change will not be easy. I don't claim to have all the answers on how to fix the system. However, I am tossing a few ideas to consider. I suggest systemic changes, not very specific proposals. Once a system starts working, it becomes proactive and can handle the details.

Political Donations: Corporations should be legally prohibited from making political donations to parties directly or through PACs. The laws should have penal provisions for corporations routing money through employees, vendors, and the like. Individuals should be free to donate via bank, with an upper limit of, say, $1,000, with cash donations not being permitted. If people, even in the most remote places, can pay for things via digital means such as UPI, why not donations?

Government Funding of Political Parties: Parties should get an annual grant from the government. This should be based on the number of votes polled for them in the last election, not the number of seats won, as this skews the actual support base. Trust me, the expense incurred by the state (people) will be far less than the savings made directly and indirectly by society.

Corporatization Of Political Parties: Since they are getting government funding, parties must be run like corporations with compliance, audits, balance sheets, and tax returns with minimal tax rates of, say, 1%. Like any corporation, they should pay salaries to party functionaries and members, motivating bright people to pursue this as a career. This will also reduce the mystical grip of dynasties on opaquely run national political parties and allow genuine and fresh talent to emerge.

Proportional Representation: At national and state levels (simultaneous polls), parties gain seats in the legislature *in proportion to the votes they receive*, ensuring fairer representation for smaller political groups. The party then decides who to send to the legislature. This will also reduce the influence of local strongmen with criminal antecedents who are often nominated due to the winnability of a particular constituency. Of course, the individual charismatic leaders continue to campaign and garner support for their parties and their policies, thereby building their influence in the party.

The 'First Past the Post' system creates a misleading impression of the amount of support the winning party may have. It also gives undue power to the winner to push their agenda throughout the state, although many people may not want it. Voices of dissent are quickly put down by the brute force of the majority in the legislature. At city and town levels, representational democracy can work well because the people need to be in touch with local leaders directly.

Direct Democracy: Elements of direct democracy should be introduced so that people can securely vote online for policies. This idea might not work perfectly, as the UK's referendum shows. However, we can start with small changes in cities and towns. As people become more experienced and informed, letting everyone vote directly on issues can make the system work better and rely less on elected representatives.

Decentralization: Decentralize power by granting more authority and resources to local or regional governments to manage local affairs more effectively. Smaller operations are naturally so much easier to manage.

Citizens' Laws: Citizens or groups should also be permitted to propose laws that the government should consider, provided they have a minimum number of proposers.

Protection of Civil Servants: Civil Services personnel must have a fixed minimum tenure. Politicians' power to transfer civil servants should be curtailed, with a Civil Services Board deciding on a (politician's) complaint.

Transparency in Policy: Government plans and policies, except those of national security, should be freely available on the websites of the concerned departments. This will remove the advantage crony capitalists have by way of selective advance information.

Transparency in Procurement: Government procurement, other than defence and national security, must be transparent, with all processes, internal files, tenders, specifications, corrigendum's, bids, and awards available live online for anyone to access. The right to information (RTI) is still being misused by authorities, who sometimes refuse to acknowledge requests or simply obfuscate facts.

Bar-On Stock Trading: Politicians (and bureaucrats) must be barred from buying or selling individual stocks directly or through persons in concert while in office. If there was ever an insider, it was the person at senior levels of the government. Exceptions must be made for index and mutual funds and the sale of stocks held before taking office.

Bar-On Property Trading: Politicians (and bureaucrats) must be barred from buying or selling land or property directly or through persons in concert while in office. They have inside information on all the plans, and their office would make many. Exceptions must be made for REITs and the sale of property held before taking office.

Unwrapped Wishes

Wealth & Inequality

Poverty is a vicious cycle that's very hard to break. Rich people keep getting richer, while poor people often have few opportunities. Wealthy individuals and big companies have more influence over politics, which can lead to rules that favor them—like policies that protect corporate profits or lower taxes for the rich. In many countries, tax rules give the wealthy an advantage by taxing money earned from investments at lower rates than money earned from work. This means that those who already own assets can build wealth much faster than those who rely only on their salary.

As economies focus more on finance, wealth becomes tied to investments, stocks, and assets instead of just work. This makes it easier for rich people to make more money, while those without money to invest fall further behind. Technology also creates significant wealth for those who own or develop new innovations, widening the gap between rich and poor.

Globalization has allowed companies to move jobs to countries with cheaper labor, leaving low-skilled workers in richer nations unemployed or underpaid. As a result, wages for some workers stagnate, while corporations and highly skilled workers continue to benefit.

Access to quality education varies significantly across socioeconomic groups, making it harder for people in lower-income brackets to access high-paying jobs. Without skill-building opportunities, people from poorer backgrounds are often confined to low-wage employment.

So, how can we reduce the disparity? Some of the reforms we can introduce are in the following areas:

Progressive Tax Reforms: Money earned from work is presently taxed at a higher rate than money made from investments, especially for high earners. In many countries, income taxes can go up to 37%, while long-term gains from investments are taxed at a maximum of 20%. This means that people who earn wages often pay more in taxes than those who make money through investments. As a result, the rich—who mostly earn from investments—can build their wealth faster, while the working class ends up with a heavier tax burden.

One way to address this is by taxing capital gains at the same rates as regular income, reducing the gap between labor and investment earnings. Some countries, like Denmark, already tax capital gains closer to income tax rates. Another approach could involve making capital gains taxes progressive so higher earners pay more or requiring investments to be held for extended periods to qualify for lower tax rates. Raising capital gains taxes closer to the levels of labor income taxes could help reduce inequality, even if it doesn't eliminate the disparity.

Unrealized Capital Gains are a clever way to disguise and evade taxes. Many wealthy individuals and entrepreneurs use stocks and other assets as a smart way to avoid paying high taxes. Instead of receiving a salary taxed as income, they get paid in stocks or hold their wealth in investments. They can then claim they have little or no taxable income because their wealth exists as "unrealized gains" — the increase in value of their stocks or assets that haven't been sold. Since taxes are only owed when assets are sold, they avoid paying taxes on this growing wealth.

Despite this, they can borrow large sums of money against their stocks or other assets. Banks treat these assets as valuable collateral, even though they are technically "notional" until sold. Borrowing against these assets allows them to fund their lifestyles, buy property, or reinvest without anything of sale—and crucially, without triggering taxes.

This strategy creates a tax loophole that favors the wealthy. The working class, who earn wages and don't have access to these mechanisms, pay a much higher share of their income in taxes. A way forward is the Periodic Wealth Gains Assessment (PWGA) Framework.

Who It Applies To: The PWGA targets very rich individuals—those whose total unrealized gains on investments exceed a high threshold (for example, $10 million). This means it only affects the wealthiest, not small investors.

Assets Included: The framework covers assets that can be easily traded, like stocks, bonds, and mutual funds. For assets that are harder to value, a standard method will be used. Taxpayers can challenge these valuations if they believe they're incorrect.

How Valuation Works: The value of the assets is updated periodically (say, once a year) based on current market prices. If the market value drops, taxpayers can carry forward the losses to offset future gains.

Tax Rate: A low annual tax rate is applied to the unrealized gains (gains that exist on paper but haven't been sold yet). This helps avoid cash flow problems while still ensuring that the wealthy contribute over time.

Avoiding Double Taxation: When an asset is eventually sold, the tax already paid on its unrealized gains will be credited, so the owner isn't taxed twice on the same gain.

Deferred Payment Options: If a taxpayer cannot sell an asset without causing financial hardship, they can choose to pay the tax later (with interest). The tax liability will be attached to the asset until it is sold.

Minimum Wealth Tax: A minimum tax that combines both income and unrealized gains might be introduced. This measure is designed to reduce tax avoidance by preventing the shifting of assets to avoid taxes.

Land Holding Restrictions: The wealthy have invested considerable sums in land and real estate holdings, with Wall Street entering this area and buying millions of homes of late. This results in skyrocketing land prices, which makes it beyond the reach of the younger generations and the people with meager means. They cannot afford to buy land to build their homes, industries, and the like and are at the mercy of the landlords. Individuals must not be permitted to hold more than a limited number of housing units. The state and the city have invested and created this infrastructure for housing its citizens, not for hoarding and profiteering. Corporations must not be permitted to buy residential housing space for holding and rent. If the capitalists find this blasphemous, they could take the opinion of their young adult children.

One way the state can make land accessible at an affordable cost is to create high-speed rail and road networks to remote places. This will also create large-scale rural employment and reverse the burden on cities. The world can learn much from China's great strides in this area.

Corporate Governance Reform: Corporations are built by the shareholders and the people who operate and run them. Sure, shareholders have a risk that the employees do not have, but the fact remains that majority owners can skew the salaries and wages to maximize profits at the cost of the employees. In publicly owned companies, there should be a maximum limit on the ownership of the promoters and a minimum share should be compulsorily held by the employees. This will give workers a voice in company decisions like profit-sharing and wages to help ensure that the benefits of corporate success are shared among all stakeholders, not just shareholders and executives.

Financial Literacy Programs: I've always wondered why the education system does not teach all high school students the basic skills required in life, such as banking, saving, investing, and insurance. This can indeed lead to better personal wealth management and economic security.

Investment in Education and Skills Training: I have been educated in a state-run school, Central School, and a state-governed college, St. Stephens, and it did not turn out so badly. Expanding citizens' access to affordable education is paramount, especially in rural and impoverished areas, and the state must bear the significant burden. The wealth and capital gains tax will easily cover the cost and then some. This will also employ a substantial number of people. Sure, private institutions are areas of excellence, but they come with hefty bills that can care for only an elite minority. In any case, the affluent have access to a good education, perpetuating the divide.

Education must include trade schools and job retraining programs. Tailoring education to market needs can also equip workers for jobs in growing industries, helping them secure higher-paying positions. This will become even more relevant in the coming years when AI largely makes many purely intellect-based professions substantially redundant.

Minimum Real Living Wages Laws: The concept of a 'minimum real living wage' refers to a wage level high enough to cover basic needs—such as food, housing, healthcare, transportation, and education—for workers and their families, providing a decent standard of living. Unlike a minimum wage, which is often a legal baseline that may not reflect actual living costs, a living wage is adjusted based on the cost of living in a specific area. It's designed to enable workers to live with dignity and avoid poverty traps. Currently, employers are getting away with paying only the bare minimum set by the state, which has often been unchanged for decades. In the United States, the federal minimum wage has been set at $7.25 per hour since 2009, while the cost of living has skyrocketed. Although some states like California and Washington and cities like Seattle and New York have higher wages, they are not close to a real living wage. This should be implemented for corporate workers and workers in the unorganized sector, such as domestic servants and drivers. I would happily see the rich buy one less BMW and pay their employees fairly. To set a minimum real living wage, the state can do the following:

1. *Set Standards Based on Local Costs*: Study the cost of living in different areas and use this information to set a fair minimum wage for each region.

2. *Enact Legislation*: Pass laws that require employers to pay at least the living wage. These laws could be introduced gradually so businesses have time to adjust.

3. *Offer Incentives for Compliance*: Give tax breaks or subsidies to companies that pay a living wage, which can be especially helpful for businesses with small profit margins.

4. *Ensure Regular Reviews and Adjustments*: The living wage should be regularly updated to keep pace with inflation and changes in living costs.

5. *Raise Public Awareness and Transparency*: Increase public awareness about the benefits of a living wage and ensure wage data is accessible for accountability.

Law & Justice

The justice system faces many challenges that differ worldwide, and in many places, people have lost trust in the courts. When courts lose their independence, society suffers because trust in the legal system and the rule of law weakens. If courts are seen as biased or politically influenced, people start to doubt whether justice is truly fair. This can create social divisions, as different groups may feel that their rights are at risk due to changing political winds rather than stable laws. A weakened judiciary also means that other parts of the government can gain too much power, which can harm democracy and risk marginalizing minority rights.

The Supreme Court and other courts are criticized in the United States for becoming more political. Presidents often choose judges who share their political views, and the Senate sometimes confirms or blocks these nominees based on party interests rather than their qualifications. This process affects how fairly the courts work, especially on hot-button issues like abortion, voting rights, and gun laws.

For example, abortion rulings have turned into a battleground where political parties push for outcomes that fit their agendas. The ongoing controversy over *Roe v. Wade* shows how political appointments can undermine long-standing legal principles that keep the law consistent and predictable.

Instances like the long delay in filling a vacancy with Merrick Garland in 2016, and the rushed confirmation of Amy Coney Barrett in 2020, demonstrate how the Senate can use the confirmation process to advance party goals. This politicization makes people view judicial decisions as partisan rather than fair, leading to a loss of public trust. Many believe that reforms such as setting term limits for judges or changing appointment procedures are needed to protect judicial independence and rebuild public confidence.

The Indian judicial system struggles with significant delays, with cases often taking decades, sometimes up to jaw-dropping 40 years or more, to reach a final judgment. This delay erodes public trust, denies timely justice, and clogs the legal system with millions of pending cases. The criminals lose all fear of being brought to justice, knowing they are not going to jail for decades, if at all. Meanwhile, the innocent is made to suffer endlessly for ages, going through the judicial grind without even an apology or compensation for the torture suffered. In my mind, this is simply inexcusable for a society to put a human being through and shows a complete apathy for human life by the state. These delays are primarily due to insufficient judicial infrastructure, a lack of judges, complex procedural requirements, and frequent adjournments that slow the pace of litigation. The problems are manifold:

Insufficient Judges and Infrastructure: India has the lowest judge-to-population ratios globally. Many courtrooms are under-resourced, leading to massive case backlogs. In many high courts, judges must address up to 70 cases daily! Poor guys. I would not like to be in their shoes.

Complex Procedures: Cases go through many levels of appeals, technical rules, and frequent postponements, which all add extra delays.

Deliberate Delays: Sometimes, parties use postponements on purpose to delay cases and avoid bad outcomes.

Old-Fashioned Methods: Many courts still rely on paperwork and manual record-keeping instead of using modern technology.

So what can we do?

1. *Increase Judges and Improve Courts*: Hire more judges and invest in better court facilities, especially in lower courts where most cases are pending.

2. *Simplify Procedures*: Make legal processes simpler, limit the number of postponements, and create fast-track courts for specific types of cases.

3. *Use Alternative Dispute Resolution (ADR)*: Encourage methods like mediation and arbitration to settle disputes outside of the traditional court system.

4. *Adopt Modern Technology*: Use digital case management, online filing, and virtual hearings to reduce paperwork and make the system more efficient.

Political Interference In Judiciary

Political interference is another major problem that affects the independence of the judiciary. To make the courts more independent, the following steps can be taken:

Unwrapped Wishes

1. *Reform Judicial Appointments:* Create an independent body to appoint judges based on merit and integrity rather than political interests.

2. *Increase Transparency:* Set clear, public guidelines for how judges are appointed and promoted. This helps prevent politically motivated choices.

3.. *Limit Post-Retirement Roles:* Stop or delay political appointments for judges after retirement to avoid conflicts of interest.

4. *Protect the Judiciary's Budget:* Ensure the judiciary controls its own funding, so it is not influenced by the executive branch.

5. *Strengthen Accountability:* Set up an independent group within the judiciary to handle complaints against judges.

6. *Promote Public Awareness:* Educate people about the importance of an unbiased judiciary. This helps build public demand for a transparent and independent legal system.

By addressing these issues and making these changes, the judiciary can become more efficient, fair, and independent. This will help reduce delays, make justice more accessible, and restore public trust in the legal system. As with the legal system, public trust in facts is eroding too.

Unbridled Mainstream Media

So I've stopped watching TV news. I can't stand the propaganda and drivel being churned out in the guise of news. The content borders on the inane, and it is evident that the owner has given the anchors and the channels a definite agenda. Channels are owned by large corporations with interests in other areas of the economy, generating their wealth. They want to protect their fiefdom by pushing the agendas of the politicians they control. If your media house has enabled the election of a particular party, you will be returned with favors, both in government advertisement and crony capitalism. Media is also a holy cow, the fourth pillar of democracy, so any calls for censorship will be met with significant criticism in the name of freedom of speech.

What can be done to recover the situation? Freeing news media from corporate influence and fostering true independence is challenging but achievable with specific structural and financial shifts:

Stronger Regulation of Media Ownership: Large non-media conglomerates must not be permitted to own media houses. Media conglomerates should be restricted from owning too many outlets, which can help prevent concentrated corporate influence. This could involve reintroducing antitrust laws and media ownership limits to encourage diverse ownership in media markets.

Public Funding with Oversight: Public broadcasters like the BBC or PBS can offer independent, fact-based reporting when funded through a tax, licensing fee, or government grants (without political strings). To safeguard this, oversight bodies of journalists, academics, and civic leaders, not government officials, could ensure editorial independence.

Subscription-Based Models: A shift to subscriber-supported news models allows media to rely directly on their readers rather than advertisers. This model encourages media companies to focus on quality and relevance for their paying audience, as seen with outlets like *The New York Times* and *The Washington Post* (although that has it's own issues).

Independent Fact-Checking and Editorial Boards: Even within corporate-owned media, creating independent, protected editorial boards and third-party fact-checking services can add independence to reporting. Ensuring autonomy in these groups' decisions could help avoid the influence of corporate executives or advertisers.

Unwrapped Wishes

"Antisocial" Media & The Social Divide

Social media is now totally driven by algorithms, with the app quickly learning your preferences and mindset and exposing you to extreme views. It is engineered to be addictive, leveraging psychology and technology to keep users engaged. Platforms use algorithms to learn what content resonates most, then deliver it in a way that constantly triggers dopamine in the brain—making it hard to stop scrolling. This is paired with a sense of social validation (likes, shares, and comments) that can feel rewarding, encouraging more interaction.

Everything is now either extreme left or right, and the center has disappeared. All this extremism has created such a great divide amongst people that they have started to hate the other side. It is destroying the social fabric and, if unchecked, will eventually lead to civil strife and the breakdown of society. We can already see the effects in the USA and many other countries. I'm sure the owners of social media platforms are fully aware since they have designed the algorithms, yet they ignore all the costs to society to keep raking in billions of dollars by profiting on hate. Shameful.

Preventing social media algorithms from deepening social divisions means changing policies and how platforms operate. Here are some simple strategies:

Make Algorithms Clear: Require platforms by law to explain how their algorithms work, including the rules for suggesting content. Independent audits can check how content is promoted to ensure transparency.

Give Users More Control: Allow users to adjust or even turn off recommendation algorithms. They could choose to see posts in order by time or set custom filters that show content from trusted sources.

Mix Up Content: Design feeds to include a variety of viewpoints and avoid echo chambers. For example, create "public interest algorithms" or dedicated sections for reliable sources and balanced discussions.

Set Ethical Standards: Establish independent oversight boards with experts like ethicists and technologists to review and guide the ethical use of algorithms. These boards can help develop systems that promote fairness and balanced content.

Reduce Extreme Content: Implement stricter rules to prevent extreme or polarizing content from being widely shared. Adjust algorithms to lower the ranking of content that is sensational or misleading, and favor high-quality, verified information.

Educate Users: Help users understand how algorithms shape what they see online. Platforms could offer in-app guides to explain recommendation systems, so people can make informed choices about their interactions.

Use Government Regulations: Policymakers can set standards for transparency, data sharing, and ethical use of algorithms. They can also offer incentives to encourage companies to focus on public welfare instead of just engagement metrics.

Support Alternative Platforms: Encourage community-driven social media platforms that use fair, less divisive algorithms, or prioritize user well-being. This can give users more choices and create healthier competition.

Implementing these steps can help ensure that social media algorithms promote a balanced view of the world and reduce social divisions. To do so, we would need to first address the intermingling of corporations and the government - a different conversation with just as deep roots.

Unwrapped Wishes

Nationalism, Hegemony, And The UN

Extreme nationalism can create division and conflict by making people think in terms of *"us versus them."* This can lead to prejudice, less cooperation, and fights over resources, borders, or beliefs. When countries focus only on themselves, they miss the chance to work together on big problems like climate change, poverty, and health crises.

On the other hand, if the world acts as one community, we can build peace and progress together. By sharing resources, knowledge, and ideas, countries can tackle global issues more effectively. Working together also encourages cultural exchange, mutual understanding, and economic cooperation, creating a more connected, strong, and successful world.

I greatly admire the United States — a beautiful country whose people have championed freedom of speech, innovation, civil rights, art, and commerce throughout the 20th century. However, it is odd that its foreign policies toward non-Western countries have often been poor and disappointing. After World War II, the United States became a global superpower, using its economic and military strength to shape a new world order. During the Cold War, the U.S. worked hard to stop the spread of communism, which led to military interventions and proxy wars in regions like Latin America, the Middle East, and Southeast Asia. This included wars in Vietnam, Korea, Iraq, and Afghanistan, as well as secret actions to influence or destabilize governments in places like Chile and Iran. Although these actions were often said to promote democracy or stability, they frequently resulted in long-term instability, many civilian casualties, and damaged relationships with other countries. This period shows the complicated balance between power, influence, and the unintended results of interfering in other nations.

The United Nations (UN), created to promote global peace and cooperation, has been criticized for being dominated by a few Western countries—especially the United States. The UN Security Council is structured so that permanent members like the U.S., U.K., France, Russia, and China have veto power, giving them too much control over global decisions. This setup often sidelines the voices of smaller or less powerful nations, whose opinions usually result in only symbolic resolutions with little real impact. Many argue that this imbalance lets powerful countries push their own interests at the expense of fair treatment for all, leaving most nations with little say on crucial issues like peace, security, and development.

In the future, the world is likely to become more multipolar, with emerging countries such as China, India, and other long-established nations becoming major power centers. This shift is driven by their fast-growing economies, technological advances, and increasing global influence. Unlike past power transitions marked by conflict or colonial ambitions, these emerging nations seem focused on improving life for their people through economic growth and better infrastructure rather than military power or aggression. They emphasize mutual respect, cooperation, and non-interference—values from their long civilizational histories. Their rise offers a chance for a more balanced and diverse world where decisions are made based on shared interests rather than the dominance of one group. This change can benefit everyone by bringing new ideas to tackle global problems like climate change, sustainable development, and economic inequality. For long-term stability, Western countries should welcome this shift and support a system that respects the diversity and independence of all nations.

To adapt to a more multipolar world, the UN needs to change its structure, especially within the Security Council. The current setup, with the U.S., U.K., France, Russia, and China holding veto power, reflects the power dynamics of the post-World War II era, not today's diverse global landscape. To be truly representative, the UN could add emerging powers like India, Brazil, and nations from Africa and the Middle East as permanent members. This change would ensure that key regions and perspectives are part of global decision-making. Removing or limiting veto power could also help avoid deadlocks on important issues and make the Council more responsive to current challenges.

If the UN does not evolve, emerging economies might create their own organization with fairer representation—such as an expanded BRICS group. This new body could focus on issues like development, infrastructure, and fair trade policies, working on a consensus basis without a strict hierarchy. Such an alternative organization could attract many countries that feel left out by the current system, challenging the UN's influence and legitimacy.

By adapting to be more inclusive, the UN can help prevent division and build a cooperative, stable world order that reflects the diverse needs and aspirations of all nations.

The Climate Crisis

The pursuit of better living standards and wealth has significantly impacted the environment. This is especially evident in developing countries, where efforts to industrialize and provide a decent quality of life often overshadow environmental concerns. The consequences include global warming, deforestation, pollution, loss of natural habitats, and plant and animal species extinction. I've seen this happening with my eyes in the past decades, making me deeply unhappy. Pristine mountains and seaside towns are now overcrowded with hotels and tourists, waste, and pollution. They are now almost not worth visiting.

Cities are now overcrowded concrete jungles, polluted, and unlivable. I get nightmares of sci-fi cities with concrete towers, not a single park with the only thing to do is to go for a meal and return to your hole-in-the-wall home. Ugh. Things are so much better in most cities in Western countries, such as Europe and a select few cities in the USA. They learned the lessons long ago and were unburdened by the vast population and poverty; it is high time we wake up and start addressing these urgently, or we will soon live in urban slums with an impoverished notion of "quality of life."

Historically, it seems like there are a few key reasons for degradation of our precious environment. Here are some noteworthy ones:

Economic Growth Prioritized Over Sustainability: Developing nations often prioritize rapid industrialization to boost their economies, sidelining environmental concerns. Resource-intensive industries like mining and manufacturing are key drivers of this growth. Environment preservation must go hand in hand with development, even if the latter must take a little back seat to protect the environment. Today, we are ready to kill any species, destroy any forest, degrade the coastline, and destroy marine life, all in the name of so-called development. So, what if we have smaller houses and cars, fewer new clothes, and fewer gizmos?

We must adopt sustainable development practices and focus on renewable energy, green technologies, and sustainable farming to balance economic growth with environmental preservation.

Overconsumption and Resource Depletion: Excessive consumption by individuals and industries accelerates resource depletion and waste generation, leading to pollution and ecological damage. Days into my first visit to the US and out on a trip to the mall, I was taken aback by the sheer extent of consumption and remarked to my host, "No society can consume this much and sustain itself." Do we need all these things, or is greed simply making us blind and oblivious to everything else?

We should reduce consumption by adopting the following:

1. *Promote Minimalist Lifestyles*: Encourage people to focus on needs over wants, reducing wasteful consumption. In recent years, this welcome trend

has been seen among the young population in Western countries, especially Europe. However, this has yet to catch on in developing countries where aspirational consumption is rapidly rising. We should learn from the mistakes of the West and leapfrog to a minimal, more sustainable, lifestyle.

2. *Shift to a Sharing Economy*: Carpooling, rental services, and shared resources can maximize use without increasing production. The concept of self-driving cars, which could be part of a carpool, seems an excellent idea for the future.

3. *Emphasize Product Longevity*: Support durable, repairable products and discourage disposable culture. Remember how the recyclable glass bottle was used repeatedly until it became outdated due to plastic? That did not turn out so well.

4. *Dietary Changes*: Reduce consumption of resource-intensive foods like meat and dairy. This may be anathema to non-vegetarians and the stuff of jokes. However, if they were to see the cruelty of mass-producing animals and birds for food, they would be more appreciative of the alternative.

5. *Encourage recycling, reusing, and waste reduction*: Industries should be required to adopt cleaner production techniques to minimize resource extraction. Tax benefits push the drive along the right path.

Weak Environmental Regulations: Inadequate policies and poor enforcement allow overexploitation of resources and unchecked pollution. In developing countries, these regulations are flouted to such an extent that I wonder if they even exist. Small hill station towns in India like Simla, Nainital, and Manali are now looking like urban jungles with traffic jams, hotels toppling over hills in the rain, water shortage, dust pollution, and litter in the countryside. And yet, a large population visits in bus loads during peak seasons for family holidays. Is there any state monitoring the regulations? I doubt very much. This is happening in various parts of the world.

We must enforce stricter laws and penalties on deforestation, pollution, and emissions. The state and civil society must launch large-scale afforestation programs, protect biodiversity hotspots, and create wildlife sanctuaries. In a sense, we must undo the damage caused to the environment by humans. Nature has a tremendous inherent ability to make a strong comeback; all it needs from us is to leave it alone. As I said earlier, left to me, I would get large tracts vacated (with relocation and rehabilitation) and let nature take over and restore them to their pristine state.

Poverty and Survival Needs: Many people in developing countries depend on natural resources for survival—deforestation for firewood, hunting for food, or farming on cleared land. We are quickly losing jungles, flora, and fauna. The extent of the loss of the Amazon rainforest to agriculture and raising cattle is mind-boggling. I recently went to Ranthambore Wildlife Sanctuary in Rajasthan after many years. Hotels, motels, and an overcrowded local town with hordes of people dependent on tourism for survival surrounded it. The first time I visited was in the mid-1980s, or about 45 years ago. The whole place was sparsely populated and wild to the extent that tigers used to roam the villages beyond the park. What a sea change and disappointment. Luckily, once inside the protected park, it was as beautiful as before. With alternate avenues of earning a livelihood, the pressure from tourism can be taken off. This over-dependence on tourism for survival is the bane of many countries and regions.

Dependency on Fossil Fuels: Heavy reliance on fossil fuels for energy contributes significantly to greenhouse gas emissions, exacerbating global warming. Fortunately, many countries like India have taken a big lead in this area, providing gas cylinders even in remote locations to reduce this dependency. It can be done!

We must also invest in renewable energy and subsidize and expand access to solar, wind, and hydropower to reduce dependency on fossil fuels. It may not be fully replaceable until a breakthrough like fusion energy occurs. However, every alternative avenue counts and, put together, can contribute a significant portion of the demand. Thankfully, this is one area where many countries are making serious efforts, and things look positive.

Population Growth: Rapid population growth increases demand for housing, food, and infrastructure, often at the expense of forests and ecosystems. However, a specific minimum population is essential for human survival, and declining numbers of people are bad for society. Japan, Korea, and many other countries will vouch for this fact. We must strike a balance. Ideally, a couple should have two children, resulting in a stable population. We must continue to invest in family planning programs, education, and healthcare to stabilize population growth.

Global Inequities: Developed nations often outsource environmentally harmful industries to developing countries, exploiting their resources and leaving them with environmental consequences. Fortunately, awareness is growing amongst customers and companies in developed countries, and a more equitable supply chain may emerge.

The Mental Health Crisis

Our society, economy, and culture have changed very quickly in the past 40 years, making it hard for many people to keep up. Many young adults find it difficult to handle traditional adult responsibilities like earning enough money, building long-term relationships, and starting families. It seems that many are stuck in a kind of prolonged adolescence, reluctant to step into adulthood fully. While it would be easy to blame the next generation, the fact that this is felt across society points to deeper issues. According to my observations, here are some key reasons and, characteristically, some possible solutions:

Economic Pressures and Instability: Many young people face unstable jobs, low wages, and rising costs for housing, education, and healthcare. This often leaves them with heavy debt (like student loans) and makes it hard to afford big milestones, such as buying a home or starting a family. The solution is largely governmental. (1) Introduce living wage policies so that young people can earn enough to support themselves. (2) Implement policies to make housing more affordable, like rent control or incentives for building more homes. And lastly, (3) Lower the cost of higher education to reduce the burden of student debt. Advances in online education and AI could help make quality education more accessible and affordable while simultaneously boosting the effectiveness of teaching material. Imagine an all-knowing teacher for each student ready to guide each child through whatever doubts they have.

Unrealistic Expectations: Social media often shows perfect images of success, beauty, and achievement, which makes young people expect quick results and instant gratification. This can lead to stress, anxiety, and burnout. The global nature of our world has only made each person more aware of who they are competing with and what they are missing out on. The solutions require a perspective shift. (1) Parents and educators should teach young people that success takes time and hard work. (2) Schools should reiterate the importance of balancing work and life so that achievements in career and material wealth are not seen as the only measures of a good life.

Social Isolation and Stigma: Digital lifestyles and the pandemic have weakened community connections, leaving many people feeling lonely and unsupported. At the same time, mental health issues are still stigmatized in some areas, making it hard for those in need to seek help. The only solution to this is real human connection. (1) Create community spaces and programs that encourage social connections and support networks. (2) Launch public campaigns to reduce the stigma around mental health and promote seeking help.

(3) Expand access to affordable mental health services like therapy and counselling.

Changing Cultural Norms: Traditional milestones like marriage and having children are no longer seen by everyone as the ultimate goals. Many young adults now prefer personal freedom and exploration over settling down, even though humans still need companionship and support. A lot of these views are caused by or correlate with the three issues mentioned above. Consequently, the solution similarly is also to encourage a balanced view of life that values both independence and close relationships, reminding people that lasting connections are important.

Lack of Preparation for Adulthood: Schools often do not teach practical life skills, such as managing money, regulating emotions, or resolving conflicts. This continues often in college where these skills are further tested. Additionally, overprotective parenting (helicopter parenting) can leave young adults less prepared to face challenges on their own. We must (1) revamp the education system to include lessons on real-life skills like financial literacy, emotional management, and conflict resolution. Also (2) educate parents on how to encourage independence and agency in their children rather than overprotecting them.

By addressing these issues, we can help young people better navigate the challenges of modern life and reduce the rising mental health crisis.

The Universe, Life, Science, and God

This is a tough one! Usually, I keep away. The conditioning of the human mind over thousands of years makes it almost impossible to have a rational discussion on the subject. But I'm going to jump in a way.

How big is the observable universe? To make sense of the mind-numbing scale, let's assume the Earth has a diameter of only 1 mm across (reduced by 12,742,000,000 or 12.74 billion times) or about the size of a pinhead. How big is the solar system (Oort cloud) relative to the pinhead? It's 146 miles, the distance between San Francisco and Nevada City. And on this massively reduced scale, how large is the Milky Way galaxy? About 193,300 times the distance between the Earth and the moon (239,000 miles)! The observable universe has 2 trillion (1,000,000,000,000) such galaxies. These are not uniformly spread but have groups, clusters, and supercluster chains and sheets that stretch hundreds of millions of light years across. There are black holes (regions in space where even light cannot escape gravity) with some of the weight of billions of solar masses. Neutron stars are so dense that a tablespoon of their matter weighs as much as a mountain on Earth. Then there are voids in the universe up to 2 billion light years across with very little matter as we know it. Wow. As per the Big Bang theory, all this emerged from the singularity the size of an actual pin head.

Was the big bang the beginning? Not likely. Science is grappling with newer ideas of cyclical universes and multiple universes. Ticking time is a reality for us mortals, but on the quantum level, it is another thing. It slows, becomes faster, and, in many situations, does not even exist (such as the quantum entanglement of particles or the event horizon of a black hole). There is no need for anything to have a beginning or creator (who created the creator is the logical next question), a concept we find impossible to understand because our minds are conditioned accordingly.

There has been such a great deal of scientific learning on the scale, composition, and life of the universe in the last 200 years. Yet, there are so many remaining questions. Humans have only identified 5% of the universe, which is ordinary matter. Dark energy is estimated to comprise 68% of the universe, and dark matter is estimated to 27% of the universe! There is much evidence that they exist, but science doesn't know what they are. Scientists are on the job, and the answer will be found in the following decades or centuries.

Going from the macro to the micro, things are equally fascinating. Think of the world around you: everything you see is made of atoms created by nuclear fusion in the stars. We are nothing but stardust! These atoms are like tiny building blocks. And everything around us, living or non-living, is made of atoms of carbon, nitrogen, oxygen, and other elements. Fascinatingly, our body composition is almost identical to the relative quantities of these elements in the universe. Each atom has a center called a nucleus, made of protons and neutrons. Around the nucleus, electrons zoom around, like planets around the Sun.

But if we look even closer, we see that protons and neutrons aren't solid bits. They are made of even smaller particles called quarks, which are held tightly together by a powerful force. Electrons and other leptons aren't made of anything smaller (as far as we know). We call these "fundamental" particles because they don't seem to have any parts inside them.

What's mind-blowing is that these essential pieces, like quarks and electrons, are not "things" in the way a grain of sand is a thing. Instead, they behave more like little bundles of energy. Think of them as tiny, invisible vibrations or ripples in an underlying energy field. Modern physics tells us that the smallest parts of our world are made of energy, not solid matter. They flicker in and out of existence, appearing as particles when we look closely, but they're more like waves of energy weaving the fabric of everything we know. In the final analysis, we and the world around us are nothing but energy, not matter.

Coming back to the Earth, it was formed around 4.54 billion years ago. The basic life forms appeared quickly, around 500 – 800 million years later. Self-replicating RNA molecules, basically a chemical reaction between atoms and molecules, started the process of life, most likely in the hot thermal vents deep underneath the ocean. At a certain point in Earth's early history, simple chemical building blocks combined and formed the first living cells without any living things around to create them. This process is known as abiogenesis. Over time, these first simple life forms became more complex, eventually leading to all the plants, animals, and other organisms we see today. It seems stastically likely that this process would be replicated millions of times across the immense universe.

On an interesting side note, the powerhouse of the living cell of all complex life, the mitochondria, was a free-living bacterium over a billion years ago. This was engulfed by simple cells forming a mutually beneficial relationship. Over time, the bacterium evolved into a permanent organelle of the cell, inheriting and exchanging genetic material with the host cell. This merger—once a mere survival strategy—proved so successful that it fundamentally reshaped life on Earth, making mitochondria indispensable to the cells of all eukaryotes, from tiny unicellular organisms up through plants and animals and finally to humans.

Scientists led by Craig Venter have created synthetic (lab-made) bacterial genomes and successfully inserted them into an empty cell, resulting in self-replication. Scientists have created RNA molecules that self-replicate under controlled laboratory conditions. How close are we to creating life from scratch, i.e., self-replicating single cells? It is supposed to be only 20-30 years away. If done, it could be the single most important discovery of science, answering the origin of life. The discovery of a single living organism, even a virus or bacterium, outside the Earth would have the same effect. It would be proven for once and for all that abiogenesis, or the creation of life from simple chemicals, is universal, and there could potentially be millions of extraterrestrial species, from the basic microbes to the most advanced, in the universe!

We are slowly but surely beginning to understand the universe and the life within. This has resulted from billions of man-hours and trillions in costs in research by the scientific community worldwide. It's one of the most spectacular achievements of the collective human mind.

There is something spectacular now available. AI or artificial intelligence currently and soon **Artificial General Intelligence (AGI)**. While humans share collective knowledge, the capability of a single human mind is limited, and it cannot process the vast amount of scientific knowledge that is now available. Imagine an AI system at the command of each human mind, with the combined knowledge of humanity and the sheer power of going through it in seconds. Imagine the result of millions of bright minds with this power. Human capability will skyrocket in the coming years and decades. AI has already collated all the current data and knowledge of humans, so there will be a lull in advancement for a while. However, using AI, we can generate discoveries and inventions faster in the coming years, and the knowledge pool will increase exponentially thereafter. AGI will take it to another level since it will create further improvements, not by humans. Most people are not using AI much out of ignorance of its capabilities, skepticism, or sheer force of old habits. This must change if people do not want to be left behind.

Quantum computing is another emerging path-breaking ability that will exponentially increase AGI's capability. Recently, Google announced the creation of a quantum computer that was able to perform a specific task in 5 minutes, which would take the current world's fastest computer 10 septillion years (1 followed by 24 zeros) to do or 725 trillion times longer than the current age of the universe! There are inferences that it uses parallel universes for computation. There is growing evidence that the human consciousness functions not on an atomic but a quantum level. Combined with quantum entanglement (read about this; it's too complicated to talk about here), this would imply that humans, quantum computers, and superintelligent beings from across the universe could one day start communicating on a quantum level. I'm only scared that humans are not mentally ready for this scale of technology and power. Or maybe we were always programmed for this, unfolding as part of an instruction manual. This is just my opinion, with no facts to back this up; however, given the phenomenal rise of humans, it's not outside the realm of possibility.

The universe, on a macro and a micro level, is just so bizarre that it is mind-numbing. The more science learns, the stranger it seems to be getting. There is so much disorder and very little order. It is an excellent dichotomy from the wonderful world that we see and understand: the mountains, seas, jungles, meadows, flowers, and flora and fauna. Compared to the immense understanding that science has brought us about the universe and life, all our old concepts, divisions, and beliefs are anachronist and highly simplistic, almost childlike. While many have traditionally turned to personal reflection or revered ancient texts to explain the universe's origins and life, our most profound understanding comes from scientific inquiry. We can uncover fundamental truths about our cosmos and life through systematic research, experimentation, and evidence-based methods.

When discussing the concept of God, conversations often shift from objective inquiry to debates about faith. Relying solely on faith or tradition isn't enough to justify a belief. I don't subscribe to beliefs without strong evidence. Instead, I maintain an open-minded approach: if someone can provide compelling, verifiable evidence for a claim—even one as significant as the existence of God—I am willing to reconsider my position and potentially adopt a new belief.

This perspective means I value empirical evidence and logical reasoning over untested assumptions or inherited convictions. Our understanding of such profound matters should be guided by careful examination and critical thought rather than by appealing solely to faith. A commitment to evidence-based inquiry is the most reliable path to uncovering truths about our world and the universe.

Unwrapped Wishes

Religion has been defined by many as a collective delusion which glues homo sapiens together. I agree. People confuse festivities and cultural events with religion. I enjoy these to some extent until I'm forced to act in a certain way or believe in fictional things. I don't have any problems with religion or the solace it brings to many people if it does not interfere with a peaceful society and scientific pursuit of the truth. Some people I like the most are profoundly religious and great human beings.

Being alive is a miracle, with you being one of the possible 300-400 million candidates who made that one instance or trillions altogether. It is purely by chance that you were born into a family of a particular faith or belief and indoctrinated into the same belief by your parents or society. Please don't take it as the absolute truth and fight over it. It's just not rational or logical, making it difficult for people of different beliefs to coexist and live together.

I love the scientific mind and the pursuit of knowledge. However, I have a pet peeve against scientists. They are so busy in their quest for knowledge and perhaps some arrogance that they do not have any time or inclination to explain to the rest of the population what they have learned about the universe in simple terms they can grasp. The average person remains clueless about the understanding of the past century, and his mind is occupied by the most basic and outdated concepts, unfounded beliefs, superstition, bias, and fear. That should change if humans genuinely evolve.

Having passion is one of the most important skills you can cultivate. Whether you are involved in business, politics, or any other field, passion drives you to explore new ideas and push past obstacles. It is the energy that fuels learning and growth, making even the toughest challenges seem manageable.

Passion helps you stay motivated and focused on your goals. In business, it can spark innovative ideas and lead to successful ventures. In politics, it can inspire you to make a real difference and work for the betterment of society.

When you enthusiastically pursue your interests, you improve your own life and inspire those around you.

Remember, passion is not something you are born with—it is developed through curiosity, practice, and a willingness to take risks. Explore different subjects, ask questions, and be open to learning new things. This commitment to growth is the key to a happy, successful, and fulfilling life.

Made in the USA
Columbia, SC
21 March 2025